"Fasten your seatbelts, Stefan is going to take you for a wild ride. It's a new and provocative dimension."
BO ÖSTEN JOHANSSON
President
The Association of Swedish Advertisers

"Straightforward thinking. It's thought-provoking. He's taking the Peppers' One-to-One philosophy a ste[p] forward."
BRAND REPUBLIC

"Totally crap!!!"
ANONYMOUS CRITIC

"Very few hear the music when they read the notes. Good examples for his theories."
MARIANNE REUTERSKIÖLD
President
The Swedish Marketing Federation

"This book lets me travel from imagination to practical experience."
JÖRGEN WAHL
CEO
Advisory Board

"Amusing case studies"
BRAND CHANNEL

WWW.DETECTIVEMARKETING.COM

Stefan Engeseth has been called everything from consultant to chaos pilot. A well-known lecturer and writer, Stefan has built a solid reputation as a sort of "Jonathan Livingston Seagull" of the business world.

Over the years, he has worked with such diverse companies as Letsbuyit.com and the Swedish Postal Service.

He has held over 500 lectures and workshops internationally at corporations and academic institutions attended by the University of Stockholm, Pace University (New York), IIU, IIR, BMW, J. Walter Thompson, Leo Burnett, DaimlerChrysler, Ericsson, Berghs School of Communication, Public relations and Pharmacia Corporation.

He has also taken part in the Öresund Consulate's reference group on the Öresund bridge between Sweden and Denmark – one of the largest projects of its kind in Europe.

He writes articles for international business magazines.

WWW.DETECTIVEMARKETING.COM

10 TIPS FOR BECOMING MORE CREATIVE

1 Hire people who have different talents than you.

2 Install a random control in the elevator so that everyone ends up on the wrong floor. Get a head start by pressing the wrong button today.

3 Exchange Filofaxes with each other.

4 Bring your children to work.

5 Invite your customers to participate in projects at an early stage.

6 Invite someone from the street to attend your next meeting.

7 Mix people in meetings: for example sales people and marketing people.

8 Change the setting of the meeting. Why not hold your next meeting at a kindergarten?

9 Create imbalance. Stand on one leg during a meeting and seek imbalance. Seek imbalance in the marketplace.

10 Use simple language. A good idea thrives on simplicity.

11 Read this book and do a little more than what's on the list.

"Stefan Engeseth crackles with energy in his book Detective Marketing. He's not afraid to think differently and he does so with the authority of long practical experience. We all need the fresh breeze that blows through this book. I recommend it wholeheartedly."
Per Frankelius, PhD Economics, Örebro University, the International School of Economics, Jönköping

"Stefan managed to distil years of experience and the ideas that inspire him into an accessible, digestible form. Detective Marketing is a book to which one turns to catch Stefan's inspiration. It gives you room to think through to your own outcomes and never dictates, making it thankfully a far more interactive title than a traditional textbook."
Jack Yan, CEO, Jack Yan & Associates

"I can't remember the last time I read such a thin book with so many memorable ideas. His ONE idea is brilliant. Stefan has an ability to put his finger on what is essential and discover new paths."
Ola Feurst, PhD Economics, Stockholm University, School of Business

"Stefan presents wild thoughts that are really wild until someone earns a fortune by using them."
Ib Lenneke, Advisor, the IBIDEA company

"Suggestions for increasing your creativity"
The Chicago Sun-Times

"His ideas are a radical 2000's evolution"
All About Branding

"Swedish business bible"
Brand Strategy

WWW.DETECTIVEMARKETING.COM

Stefan Engeseth

DETECTIVE MARKETING™

Third Edition

WWW.DETECTIVEMARKETING.COM

Stefan Engeseth Publishing
tel/fax +46 (0)8 651 44 54
www.detectivemarketing.com
info@detectivemarketing.com

Art direction and layout: Layograf / Jonas Nilsson
Cover design: Forsling & Flyborg
Illustrations: Magnus Eriksson
(page 110: Max Eriksson, age 4)
Illustration: J.Nordwall Design /
Joachim Nordwall (page 75-76, 123-125)
Illustration: Nofont / Andreas Carlsson (page 116-117)
Illustration: Forsling & Flyborg (page 143)
Cover photo: Thomas Svensson
Third edition revised and re-worked by Steve Strid
Per Nilsson re-worked chapter common sense in branding
Digitally printed in the UK & USA by Lightning Source
Third edition
ISBN: 91-631-1389-9

TABLE OF CONTENTS

FOREWORD BY JAN CEDERQUIST

Co-Founder of Hall & Cederquist, part of the Young and Rubicam Group

Stefan Engeseth is a rare bird in the marketing jungle. He flies free like Jonathan Livingstone Seagull and calls himself a "chaos pilot". This naturally entails risk, but it also means that he sees more than the singing canaries who are just wise enough to look out of their cages to see the world has vertical stripes.

Engeseth hasn't been blessed with this sort of wisdom. His world view hasn't been steeped and stiffened by higher education, which means he is perpetually curious and eager to learn. The common sense in his book has grown from what he has experienced and learned during his flights through a reality far from the fettered world of academic dissertations. This is a definite advantage in a world changing so quickly that those who take an afternoon off fall behind the times.

This is basically a book about creativity. Everyone has experienced creative flashes. Everyone chases creativity, that elusive ingredient, so essential and so exciting. Yet, no one can define it. The shelves of books written on the subject bring us no closer to an answer. Nor does this book. What it does succeed in doing is bringing us closer to that gut feeling that is the source of all creativity.

Almost everyone can ride a bike, yet no one can explain how it's done. You can give an exact description of what's involved in "counteracting the tendency to fall by turning the handlebars so that the arc of each turn for each given angle of imbalance is diametrically proportional to the speed of the bicycle squared". Engeseth doesn't waste his breath on angles and curves (at least not mathematical ones). He talks about riding a bicycle, or preferably flying, as a way of getting somewhere.

Enormous amounts of money are invested in marketing. Yet, how much wins the favor of the market and how many brands win a place in the mind of the consumer? Much of the noise you hear from the marketplace is the sound of money being flushed down the toilet, even money that was spent following every rule in the book for reaching the right target group with the right message.

The science of marketing is essential for success. Essential, but not sufficient. Why did Levi's jeans suddenly start collecting dust on store shelves after years of being a natural part of every fashion-conscious consumer's wardrobe. It could hardly have anything to do with the marketing. There was nothing wrong with the jeans. Something else happened out there in Consumer-Land. For some reason, the Levi's hypnosis lost its power on the collective unconscious.

This is the great challenge for everyone involved in marketing: people are still a mystery. We know very little about human behavior. We don't even understand how communication between two people really works, let alone mass communication. Communication is part words, part body language, part tone. As for the rest, we haven't a clue. How then, are we supposed to communicate between a company and a target group?

No matter how much you know about "the angle of imbalance is diametrically proportional to the speed of the bicycle squared", it doesn't mean you know how to ride a bicycle.

Getting somewhere on a bicycle takes another kind of experience altogether as does getting somewhere in the marketing jungle. Logic and rational thought can take us part of the way. The rest requires intuition, creativity, empathy and other intangibles that can't be packaged in square, easily stacked boxes.

It is somewhere at this altitude you will find Stefan Engeseth flying. If you hold onto your hat and come along on a flight you may just land with something new in your baggage.

Jan Cederquist

AUTHOR'S FOREWORD

This Book Depends on You!

I have written this book in a very concentrated form. It's up to you to add water to your own taste.

This book is based on my experience in sales and marketing. The book is meant to bring together people with different backgrounds, help them understand one another and find ways of using their know-how to reach better results in their professions. All too often, I have seen creativity and cooperation surrender to the notion that people just cannot understand one another. My thoughts on bringing people together I've developed into a method I call *Detective Marketing*.

Calling on my experience as a sports coach, my message is built on what is inside you, your skills and experience. You, my reader, are my raw material. In cooking, the result is often dependent on the quality of the ingredients. Such is the case in this book. You are the basis of the message and the value of the book is how you interpret its contents. Having the courage to face the unexpected with an open mind and an open heart is a prerequisite to understanding this book and its method. It is when you can transfer the message to your own reality that you will see a larger picture and there you will hopefully find what you are looking for. Use your inner child and you will remove all obstacles to the future.

This book is based on my theory of creative business and the meeting of minds. Because this requires a certain mindset from the reader, my readers are primarily professionals in IT, PR, corporate communications, advertising, marketing and sales. Creativity, however, knows no boundaries. No matter what your profession is, Detective Marketing can help you grow.

About the Author

Many call me a chaos pilot, in which case this book is my request for a landing permit for innovation. I like to think of myself as a student of life. As a student, I write articles, lecture, teach, socialize with interesting people and learn through mentors. My marketing experience comes from a number of advertising agencies and e-commerce companies. I'm a self-made entrepreneur, the library is my university and southern Sweden has been my college of common sense.

I've held hundreds of lectures at corporations and academic institutions attended by The University of Stockholm, Pace University (New York), J. Walter Thompson, Leo Burnett, McCann-Erickson, DaimlerChrysler, Ericsson, BMW, Skanska, Associations of Advertisers and Marketing Federations in different countries, IIR, SEB, Public relations- and Pharmacia Corporation, ICL and Statoil. I've held thousands of workshops for all kinds of companies. I also took part in the Öresund Consulate's reference group on the Öresund bridge between Sweden and Denmark – one of the largest projects of its kind in Europe.

I write articles for international business magazines. My most valuable experience, however, is what I've learned from everyday life and the people I've met along the way. This is why I'm looking forward to meeting you in this book.

Why a Book?

"Knowledge shared is knowledge doubled" is the theme of this book. The method is called Detective Marketing and is described in the first chapter. I began my writing career ghost writing for others, until I decided it was time to develop my own thoughts. That was in 1996 when I thought a thin book would take a couple of weeks to write. Six years later, I've started to understand what Mark Twain meant when he said "I apologize for writing such a long letter. I didn't have time to write a short one."

After years in marketing, I've met many different people with different skills. What I've seen too little of is a meeting of minds between these people. Close cooperation, for example, between marketing and sales people creates new opportunities for both. I am convinced that Detective Marketing can even be used by a wide variety of groups where working together can open up new doors. It has been my goal in this book to show what you can create using my method.

IT is becoming an increasingly visible arena where people with different backgrounds meet and thrive on the resulting synergy. Getting the most out of new technology requires new ways of working. Detective Marketing can help create a fusion of different companies into a new corporate culture. When two companies meet in the light of their differences, a new culture is born and begins to grow.

Detective Marketing is all about searching, creativity and communication between sender and receiver, two people who are just waiting to meet.

A Meeting of Minds Creates New Opportunities for Growth

History shows that when two cultures meet, the result is often a great leap forward. There are bridges being built all over the world, both within countries and between them. I am convinced that the mental world opens up as a result of the opening of the physical world. Bridges between schools, research areas and the corporate world have shown the benefits of working together towards a common goal.

My goal is that Detective Marketing will help you build your own bridges between your skills and the skills of others.

As a believer in complete interactivity, I see a natural dialog with you, who I am happy to say, are going to read this book. I would love to hear your opinions at *www.detectivemarketing.com*. Think of this book as an expedition on foot that leads to my homepage.

Welcome to an inspiring meeting of minds!

Stefan Engeseth

1
Background and Methodology

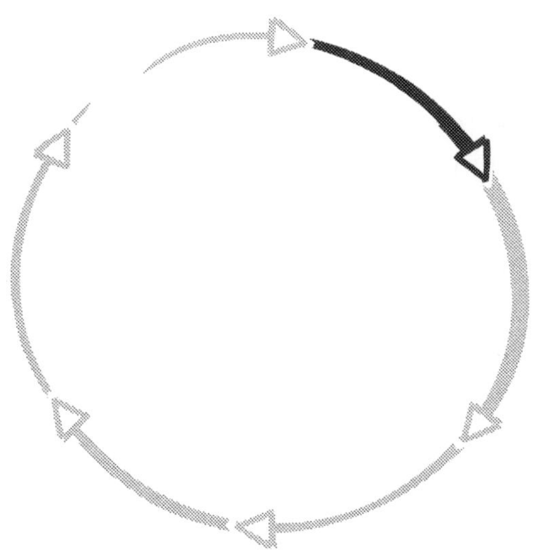

Everyone has heard the expression: "There's nothing new under the sun" which I have interpreted to mean: "See things in a new light and you'll see a new world of opportunities." Detective Marketing will help you see these opportunities. One question I often ask myself is if the helicopter could fly long before Leonardo Di Vinci saw it. It's all about seeing opportunities.

Detective Marketing is like building bridges to creativity. A bridge gets its strength from the materials from which it's built and the tension between them. This will be the basis of our bridges as well. The building materials will be developed in this chapter along with the dynamics of my method. From there, we will explore different ways of keeping creativity alive, such as search processes, the "G-customer" and other tools for success.

When one becomes two, a family is formed, something we can all relate to since we are all results of a sort of creative moment. This is the basic formula for all bridge-building: 1+2=4.

Factor 1 meets factor 2 and gives birth to an additional factor (1). Together these three factors become a family (4). Two plus one doesn't equal three, but four, because the family is a new way of thinking, a new set of values to grow with. Giving birth to each other's ideas means that everyone grows.

Models help give things structure, but not content.

How you define things is up to you, what's important is that you work towards clear goals without getting stuck in the models I offer as examples. These models are merely meant to give you a helping hand in your development. Simplicity must always be a guiding light.

A Bridge Consists of Building Material (x-axis)

A bridge consists of various different materials. The materials complement each other for maximum strength. A good meeting results in the same kind of strength. The different parties complement each other; there is meaningful give and take. Start by making a list of what type of "material" you have brought with you: sex, age, education, etc. There is strength in diversity, yet it is all too common that people hire people with similar talents instead of different ones. This leads to administration rather than growth.

Dynamic Tension Holds the Construction Together (y-axis)

By building a bridge to an unknown land you are shaping the future. All bridges are built with a

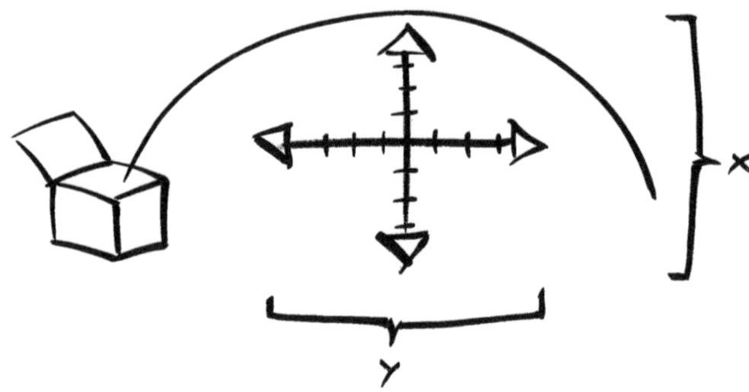

certain amount of balanced tension. Tension in bridges is never constant, but rather is constantly in motion. The tension in a meeting is created through inspiration, personal dynamics, chaos, role-playing, etc.

And remember to leave your box and take off your mask. Seek out opposites from other fields, educational backgrounds, frames of references and values. Being conscious of your own "box" is a great asset in meeting others.

The Interplay of X and Y

Two different sets of skills together form a third – the supporting structure of the bridge. Combining the x and y axes puts others' frames of reference in perspective and helps you create your own new patterns. Together, we can create common goals and work towards them. Break through the barriers of the ordinary! Build each other up and everyone's creativity will thrive. Your goals will give you all a feeling of reaching new heights, making everyone's climb that much easier. Find the "heights of creativity" that are right for you. But don't forget the walls – the creative room should be seen in terms of space as well as height. The meeting of opposites will result in new meetings in uncharted regions.

The dynamics involved can also be interpreted by the intensity of emotion involved. For example, the menu of a Turkish restaurant in my neighborhood is dedicated to "building bridges between different cultures". There is a quote on the menu that reads: "If you wish to build a bridge to the hesitant, don't give him gold, don't shower him with presents. Win him over with your cooking." In other words: by sharing experiences you create new experiences for both parties.

Simplicity is the key to not losing focus. Let the length of the two axes complement each other so that the tension between the two can hold the bridge together. The idea that carries the most weight is often very simple. Use role play – create real or hypothetical situations. How is the group affected? What values should be discussed? Feel free to swing back and forth from inspiration to solutions. Use common sense to see the big picture in the little. Use curiosity, openness, common and different reference points. See the small details to understand the big picture.

The models in this book have been kept simple to avoid getting stuck in theory. Interpret them as freely as you like, as long as they lead to productive development. There are no right or wrong ways, only an opportunity to grow.

Creative Passion

All creativity is connected. It all requires the same devotion and energy required to create new life. The act of creating can be seen as a sort of self-realization, regardless if the creation is a child or this book. When Freud talked about our sexual needs, he envisioned a larger concept: creation. What Freud spoke of was creativity at a primal level.

Product development is both development and evolution. In the beginning, creativity was a matter of survival. Today, it's a matter of surviving in a qualitative sense. Comparing a newborn child with a new car may be a bit exaggerated; yet, an inventor feels that it's natural to call his invention his baby and in creative fields we often talk about "the birth of an idea". Renewal and development are essential. Can they be part of the same basic survival instinct?

Creative passion gives the methodology of the meeting a deeper meaning. Think of it: when do we and other members of the animal kingdom use energy most intensely? When new life is created. Creation is energy that takes on a new dimension, a sort of transformation of the present into the future.

In today's society, we no longer need to build houses to survive. We have inherited everything we need to survive: houses, farms, factories, etc. This goes against human nature. Human nature has a need to create, to build, to connect. Internet has taken up part of the need for a new frontier. Here there are many parallels to the old west – everyone can stake a claim, everyone can find new ways of making money.

When everything is organized, digital and effective the consumers start longing for the opposite. The Swedish brand "Light My Fire" use this to offer consumers dreams of romance and freedom. They sell fire (products to make and handle fire with) by using the passion from their customer's dreams.

What kind of passion is related, or could be related to your product/brand?

How can your company work together with costumers, to see and meet their needs?

Keeping the Present Alive Also Requires Creative Passion

Tension is the heart muscle of creativity.

The relationship of creation to creativity began on the day you were born. And if creation and creativity are linked, then creativity must be a true survival instinct. Evolution in the business world must therefore always be plugged into some form of creative naiveté.

A LITTLE IMBALANCE FOR A LOT OF CREATIVITY

History gives us a number of examples where meetings between different cultures and peoples have created success in art, literature and science. When people find themselves in the no-man's land between chaos and order, they discover that they are standing at a mental high ground where development comes most naturally. Chaos is not necessarily negative; chaos gives birth to tomorrow. To lose your balance is merely a way of moving towards the unexpected. The courage to lose one's footing in a meeting depends on personal chemistry. Meetings should always be documented and a decision maker should always participate in the work group. The creative meeting can be described as an inner force that tickles the intellect. Look at it as the art of losing one's balance, yet never falling. Don't be afraid of imbalance in the meeting – it can give rise to unexpected ideas and open new doors.

Resting between any two sets of skills there is always a third, a virtual skill that resides more in the stomach than in the head. Recent research has indicated that the ability to switch between different frames of reference is a component of creativity. This is exactly what I have endeavored to do with my Detective Marketing method: the meeting of your skills and frame of reference with those of others. (Research on creativity is vast in scope. When I refer to creativity in this book, I am referring to my own experiences combined with my interpretation of others' research.)

Staying abreast of the latest developments often requires more than is humanly possible for someone without a staff of twenty. One advantage of Detective Marketing is that it makes it possible for different fields to work together. For example: a taxi driver in City X knows City X, but not City Y, while the opposite applies to a taxi driver in City Y. Together, they can not only find more places in both cities, but also in other places such as region Z.

Don't let your own experiences cast a shadow that keeps you from seeing what you don't understand. If it feels good, it is!

Let Common Sense Set the Agenda

We are all human beings. Take off your mask – your title, position, technical jargon and everything else that is an obstacle to communication. Meet each other face to face.

Use games and role-playing. Body language makes it easier to tune into each other's wavelengths and understand each other's thoughts. Role play leads to participation that increases the ability of the individual to create. Role play gives a mirror image of your own role and opportunities. Dare to drop your mask and you will grow. Different skills can create imbalance which leads to movement and change.

Standing up during the meeting is a good way of getting started. Seek creative stimuli in both the internal and external environment by holding the meeting in inspiring places. Choose conference facilities and activities that encourage a creative mindset. Being outdoors is often a good idea as are frequent changes of setting.

If you are working as a group, "ignorance" should be made an important part of the collected skills of those present. Knowledge can be intolerant while ignorance can sometimes encourage untried new ideas. The untried idea is an important part of Detective Marketing. It is easy to dismiss the opinions of people who are unfamiliar with the specialized language of a field as ignorant and unintelligent, but their perspectives and ideas, although a little rough around the edges, can often be new and exciting.

It is also important to have a certain distance to one's own knowledge. You don't always know best. And even if you do, there are always viewpoints that are worth noting. In meetings between several generations, it is often difficult to understand each other's experiences, but these meetings can often lead to real growth.

Work with yourself. What resources do you see? What weaknesses? Ask someone to describe you.

Collect and record the group's individual characteristics such as cultural background, sex, interests, etc. See each other's differences as the group's most important resource. Analyze which seeds you wish to sow, what ideas you wish to work with and "give away" the ideas that your group doesn't wish to pursue. An idea that doesn't fit in your work, may work just fine in another part of the company. Don't keep ideas to yourself, they need other perspectives to grow. Be humble towards other's ideas, generous with your own.

Creativity as a Driving Force

For me creativity isn't just a driving force, it's an addiction. If I bottle up my creativity, my entire body shakes with negative energy. If I let my creativity flow, it feels infinite. This intoxicating feeling has been described by many people in many different terms. One familiar word is "flow". I prefer to call it life. Working methodically in a group and reaching a collective flow I call "super-flow". Creative joy shared is creativity doubled and then some. Creative joy gives better results and fewer ego problems. Always strive for super-flow!

Creativity, rush, flow, life – whatever you chose to call it – it is an essential part of all work. The ability to turn ideas into reality creates motivation. Conversely, when the ideas cannot be realized, negative feelings and anxiety are created. The result is anything but creative.

Childish Simplicity

Throughout this book, I will give a number of concrete examples. The book's value and relevance will increase in proportion to your ability to see your own opportunities in these examples.

Don't lock up your creativity. Think of what a child would do. A child sees opportunities with wonderful ease. Let this positive energy create a stimulating rush of creativity. Children act as creative consultants when you play with them. Make the most of this free, but invaluable consulting time! In the world of imagination, a child visualizes his creativity by turning dreams into mental images for the here and now. As adults, we tend to normalize our visions. We quiet them down and housebreak them. The imagination is full of possibilities; let us make our visions just as rich. The presence of children stimulates creativity. Why not schedule the next board meeting at a day care center? Read more in *Lessons from the Sandbox* (Gregerman, 2000) to utilize the magic of childhood for inspiration in your business life.

One of my most influential mentors is named Erik. Erik is 3 years old and can be seen interviewed on this book's website. See this film together with other consultants Erik's age and discuss.

On a platform in between reality and illusion there is no right or wrong. How can this increase tolerance for the "undone" in the creative meeting?

Applied Humility

"No one is perfect, not even me".

Use this sort of introduction to open a formal meeting and you will open doors to innovation.

The informal meeting is important. It is here participants learn about each other. It is better to place one piece of the puzzle at a time and understand why it goes where it goes, than getting large parts at long intervals. Take time to show an interest for others' opinions and questions. Acknowledgement and recognition inspires creativity. Humility and inspiration are the best basis for a true dialogue.

Dare to ask questions – "I didn't understand what you meant, could you explain it again?" Asking politely and showing a genuine interest helps get the most out of these meetings. Let the questions tickle the participants' curiosity and draw out the group's hidden resources.

Not Understanding is The Easiest Form of Knowledge

Work consciously to create an atmosphere where everyone is comfortable. Use humor. Do not let the meeting become a forum for grievances. It is so much easier to criticize the ideas and suggestions of others, than it is to come up with your own new ways of thinking. Concentrate on tomorrow. Conflicts can be productive and sometimes it's necessary to point out the impossible in someone else's idea. For the most part, however, this is counter-productive. When someone in the group gets a rush of creativity, a flood of ideas will come pouring forth to the entire group. Ask questions, but don't be condescending; that person is at his or her most vulnerable. Lift instead of dampen. Utilize his or her creative energy. Who knows what is possible the moment an idea is born? Let the meeting flow like a jazz jam session, where everyone is given a solo. The business community needs more jazz!

A meeting that bubbles with enthusiasm and new ideas is magic, like falling in love. Don't let egos get in the way of the feeling. The more you acknowledge each other's ideas, the more your results will improve. Collective intelligence is greater than that of the individual and besides, who wants to dance alone?

If there are participants at the meeting that see only problems, give them time. If they still are unable to adapt to this new way of thinking, they should perhaps be excluded from these meetings. Discuss where they might make a more meaningful contribution and feel more satisfied. No one feels good about constantly having to raise objections. Be firm without stepping on anyone's toes.

Judgments that hamper magic and love in creativity also dampen motivation. Wake the love of creativity and your enthusiasm will carry you towards your goals.

Ask questions and try to understand each other's ideas to allow the group to grow. Let the ideas create the content. Become a chameleon of the meeting who plays a number of different roles. If you have a tendency to be too verbal and domineering you can ask the other participants questions to encourage them to be more active. Put value on silence; silence can also be very creative. Seek chaos and confusion. Seek movement. Just say no to passive coffee sipping.

You'll soon find a format that you feel comfortable working with. Look at change as a long-term process with many steps. You can't accomplish everything in one single meeting. You are the only expert on what form your meeting will take. Discuss what tomorrow should look like.

Remember, it is the combination of sun and rain that causes a seed to grow.

METHODOLOGY – STEP BY STEP CHAOS

Someone once asked me if I had a formula for creating new ideas. I thought about the question for quite awhile, trying to define how I "get an idea". My formula turned out to be 1+2=4. A given factor (1) is added to another given factor (2). Normally, the sum would be 3, but for an idea to shine yet another factor must be added making the answer 4. (1+2=3+1=4)

Detective Marketing contains the following three parts or models: the idea that is created in the creative meeting, the process of searching and the process of investing in relationships (the G-customer). In the following pages, I will describe these three parts and illustrate them with a number of hypothetical examples. Work with these models, then simulate the reality you wish to change and mould it into what you would like to see in the future.

This method is based on people having the courage to meet between different areas (1 and

2). When different fields and know-how meet, a new dimension is created. The methodology develops organically using key words from the meeting between factor 1 and factor 2. The result is described as factor 4. Factor 4 is the new dimension created when there is a true meeting of minds.

The dimension that exists just "between the skills of two people" is virtual rather than constant. Between the skills of any two people, there is a third set of skills which I call "virtual skills". Virtual skills means that your results will always be unique. The result, 4, is the goal of your creative work.

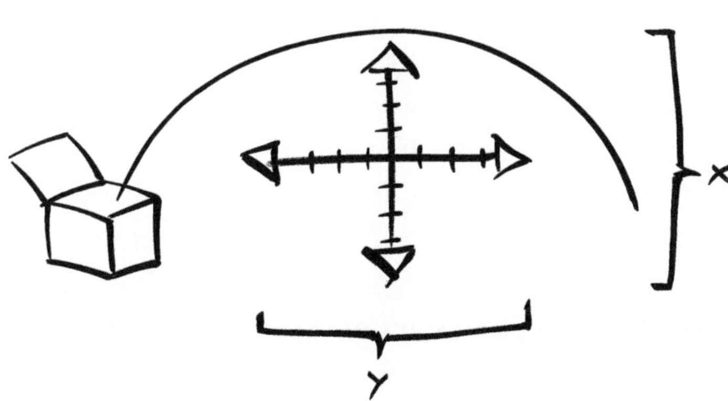

Up on the high bridge, the meeting creates a new dimension. The meeting can be between two people, products or anything else that can result in progress. Let the meeting's creative potential steer your work, from creativity to feasibility. Use simple language to avoid misunderstandings. Tear down the iron curtain of language and make it easier to work together. Identify the problems to be solved. *Focus on the possibilities.*

Draw a circle around the area where creativity must be translated into results. Try to see the big picture by taking time to look out from the high bridge. "Where on the market do we see opportunities, needs, problems, change? What know-how do we have, both visible and hidden. Where are we looking for answers? What customers can we make part of the process?"

A broadened perspective is like a magnifying glass. A magnifying glass lets us shift the focus to new areas on the market. Identify the essential points through two-way communication with selected customers. If the market doesn't see a value in what you are suggesting, perhaps it doesn't have any. Never lose sight of the big picture and structure routines accordingly.

The companies and industries that have the ability to change their perspective, scan the horizon to see their product development with new eyes and thus succeed in producing good products and services, develop highly specialized and successful know-how.

Those who succeed in bringing together divergent points of view and create something entirely new, have a bright future. You are free to go from limitations and expectations to a world of possibility.

The pattern you see helps you make sense of the past, present and future.

Creating an image of tomorrow means constantly updating and restructuring information about future scenarios. Active research will make it easier to find applications for the fruit of your creativity. The concrete usefulness of creativity is the message of the model. Theory does not inspire; by simulating new realities, practical models can give birth to ideas undreamed of.

Brands and company names are used in this book only to make it easier to use my methodology in daily life. The examples are hypothetical and are included here for educational purposes only.

THE DETECTIVE MARKETING METHOD

Getting meaningful results requires a strategy. This chapter will present a number of models that will help your creative work.

Original Idea – Development

Your own thoughts are the only limit to your creativity. Your participation in creative work can break any barrier regardless of what stage of development you find yourself at or what your background is.

Change is attracted to the future. Why separate the two when they'll meet just around the corner?

There is nothing remarkable about creativity. What is remarkable, however, is going from an idea to concrete results. Unfortunately, the person who gave birth to the idea is often not included in the process of realizing the idea. The idea could, in many cases, have become much more if the connection with its originator had been maintained during development. An idea is merely the tip of the iceberg. Making the creator a part of the project is the only way of knowing what is under the surface and understanding the inner dimensions of the idea. If you use only the tip of the iceberg, the idea often melts quickly and runs out into the sand.

Many ideas have succeeded without their inventor, yet who knows how far they could have gone with the "right" know-how from start to finish.

Other examples show how companies have grown around the person who had the original idea. My experience has been that it takes a certain creativity to give birth to an idea, but turning it into a reality and a success requires a different kind of creative thinking and energy. If the corporate world could see its idea bank as a way of staying in touch with the original idea, I think more ideas would succeed in the marketplace.

The Active Search Process Puts You One Step Ahead

It's common sense that if you wish to succeed, you can't sit around waiting for the market to come and ask for your product. Nor can you sit and wait for the talented people you need to give you a call. You must always search actively.

Detective Marketing lets you get to know the market through an active search process. In the magnifying glass you will see new connections and opportunities. Learn to navigate your creativity. Those searching for creativity and communication will experience the magic feeling that results when a sender and receiver meet on common ground. The magnifying glass magnifies your market and its opportunities.

The Internal Search

The skills you need may be right in the next room. Start your search internally, in your own company. Create a know-how bank. Who in the organization can find you and your skills? How can the right people find each other?

Large organizations have enormous resources in the form of hidden talents such as spare time interests, social skills, contacts, etc. An on-going active search process with frequent updating of your skills and that of your colleagues can make many of these hidden resources available to the company. IT solutions work well to this end; for example, search functions on the company intranet that make it easier for people in the company to find each other. The Swedish insurance giant, Skandia, was among the first in the world to account for human capital in its annual report along side the traditional figures. Many other companies will surely follow suit.

(After this book was published in Swedish, many large Swedish companies called me and asked about doing just that. "Why didn't we see these hidden resources before? Maybe it was just too obvious." It is always rewarding to see someone discovering the magic of seeing things a little differently.)

Searching for Product Needs

What does the market want? Where on the market can we see these needs? Marketing studies point to needs that the company can also identify by interpreting trends. By looking through the magnifying glass you will find what you are looking for and act upon what you find. For example: a consumer goes to a high-class cafe and has a memorable experience: he drinks that best espresso he has ever tasted. The need for this taste exists from the time he leaves the cafe and continues even when he comes home. This puts demands on the market to offer the consumer a reasonably priced espresso machine for home use. It can also mean a certain kind of coffee must be imported and sold by the major grocery chains. This need opens the door to new opportunities. The opportunities are already there waiting to be discovered.

Another example is a grocery store that now offers "restaurant" services and fast food along with detergent and milk. Delicious, restaurant-quality food made in the store, ready to take home and heat. The next step for the stores could be to teach their customers to cook. A guest gourmet chef could teach customers the tricks of the trade. Every action that adds value in the grocery store has profitability and growth potential. Sooner or later, everyone gets hungry!

Another example comes from questioning the world around us: What is real and what is fake? One can say that the world is really "faked up". Fake is real in a fake world. Fake is business. Why not create a trend that expresses and confirms "the fake world". Trends are not created in a vacuum. Punk culture had a very high profile in its day. Today, outrageous colored hair is more common than many would care to admit. It's easy to have twenty-twenty hindsight as to who created what when. Why not create a fad of your own, for example, wigs for men! Today, wigs for men are an embarrassing subject. Even the man who sells them would often rather be bald than use his own products. There is a parallel here with pink shirts. For years, it was very obvious that no real man would wear a pink shirt. Then came the button-down oxfords of the 80's and suddenly every man had a pink or pinkish shirt in his closet. The same could be done with wigs. The need is global and there is enough tension in the subject to create truly memorable advertising and PR. Capturing top-of-mind would be a cinch. The Bob Marley tune could be changed to "No Hair, No Cry". A bald man with "Someone stole my wig" tattooed across his shiny head could be a poster child for the new fad. I'm convinced that wigs for men could become a global fad in 14 days.

Do you feel yourself losing your balance in the example below? Do you see the path to the goal? What does this say about the society in which we live, about what is fake and what is real? Ask yourself how the following scenario would affect the introduction of wigs for you. Imagine, the Italian championship soccer team or this year's NBA champions playing in wigs. Can you name three stars that wear different colored wigs day after day. Describe how the female audience would react? Could different colors symbolize different traits such as single, divorced, likes a sense of humor? Can wigs be made to grow like plants? Could you use an Elvis wig as a trademark? Could other target groups be put in the spotlight through some kind of event? Would wigs fit into today's 70's trends? Can wigs be made in team or corporate colors? When, historically, did men wear bright wigs?

The Search for Distribution

Where does the consumer wish to consume? Brand shops is a way of countering established retailers. These shops are a way of getting closer to the consumer. Here, you can only buy one attractive brand. A further development of this idea could be "brand streets" on the Internet (a collection of brand names), such as a brand street with 7,000 jeans of different makes. Internet makes it easier to develop added value.

Meeting places can also be a form of distribution. Stockholm's subway system, for example, is one of the biggest distributors in the city. Åhléns, the largest department store chain, has built the entrance to its grocery store and music, multimedia, stationary and book departments directly connected

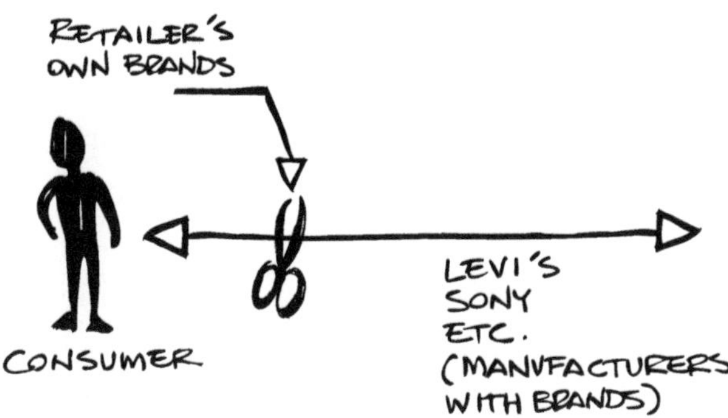

to the central station. Over a quarter of a million people a day pass by the central station, of which 50,000 enter the store.

The Search for Knowledge

Where do you find new knowledge. Education is growth; you should always see your desk as part of a classroom. The world, just like life, is ever-changing. Following change is also a sort of search for knowledge. Challenge your own conceptions and you will always find new knowledge. Meeting people with other talents, will increase your own. Start by structuring all internal and external information to encourage this sort of exchange. Try to create a self-educating organization.

Trends and events in the world should be charted in detail and followed carefully.

The Search for Customers

Headhunt your dream customers! Where are they? Choose the customers you wish to work with, then collect all the information you can about them.

By using the SPIN method of interviewing, you will get an accurate picture of who you are selling to. You will get an idea of what your product and service portfolio should contain. Your customers will become part of an positive spiral in creating a winning concept. The right customers will give your company a strong identity when your products and services become visible on the market. The right rings on the water are the key. Read more about SPIN in *Spin Selling* (Rackham, 1988).

The Search for Active Consumers

When a company, in both its advertising and on its packaging, encourages consumers to contact it with comments and questions, it gives the market a picture of the company as open and responsive. Every time your customers visit your website, an interactive platform is created. Here, you can create a database that can be used to create a more two-way communication. Once a dialogue has been created, the needs of the consumer can help set the guidelines for your communication. Being able to quickly reach your customers is an invaluable asset in the marketplace.

Many customers race around like zebras on the Internet without knowing that the stripes are actually bar codes. With today's technology, ethics and respect for privacy become important issues. Where do zebras like to be? Where do they stop to drink? Where do they seek their oases? When you've found the zebras, you can always ask them a few questions.

Active customers are often better at developing a market than companies themselves. One obvious reason is that the customer's life is affected to a larger degree by the product or service than is the company staff. Listen carefully to the comments of the active consumer. Many smaller companies use common sense and simplicity in their dialogue with the consumer. One of these is HIFI Art, a local stereo store. The owner, Kent Melin, has developed a truly unique dialogue with his customers.

I call his technique "make the customer your best salesman". It took a number of visits to his store before I realized that the salesman who was helping me wasn't a salesman at all, but rather a regular customer. The owner is at the store, but customers often find everything they need, including advice, by themselves. The more experienced customers help the new ones. The customers discuss the best brands and what the store should carry, allowing the owner to always have the right selection in stock. The customer's value grows on a long term basis. One problem with traditional customer clubs is that although they have been successful in getting customers to stay, they have been less successful in increasing their numbers. The result is a dying target group. In Kent Melin's store, customers are part of a sort of customer hierarchy, where the active customers invite the new ones into a society. Kent Melin is a visionary who lets his customers live and grow in his personal vision. With his permission, I asked his customers a few questions. The answers were very interesting, considering that many of his products are available at other stores, probably at better prices. "He carries what I want. We have the same taste...The other stores don't know what goes with what." (Read: They don't listen to their customers).

"Kent knows what I want because he knows what stereo I have at home." One customer pointed out that it's important to eat before coming to Kent's store; a visit can take 2-3 hours.

Kent Melin's personality and ability to run his store, based not only on a business idea, but also on a philosophy, seems odd at first. The more you learn about it, however, the more sense it makes.

Different solutions and opportunities are everywhere on the market. The Detective Marketing method helped me evaluate and understand Kent Melin's unique skills. When you work to build bridges to other people's know-how, your understanding for the other side of the bridge increases. Building bridges automatically teaches you humility and increases your ability to see and listen. "Everything makes sense if you can see the sense in it".

The search is never-ending. It can be compared to a computer virus that is constantly finding new ways to strike. When a hacker succeeds in getting past a large corporation's security, it shows the power of searching. The person who searches is always one step ahead in adaptability, acquiring new knowledge and foreseeing events and openings. This is no glorification of hackers and the damage they cause, it is rather a way of emphasizing the strength of the searching process.

Begin the search process by asking yourself what information you need. Structure your work accordingly and evaluate regularly.

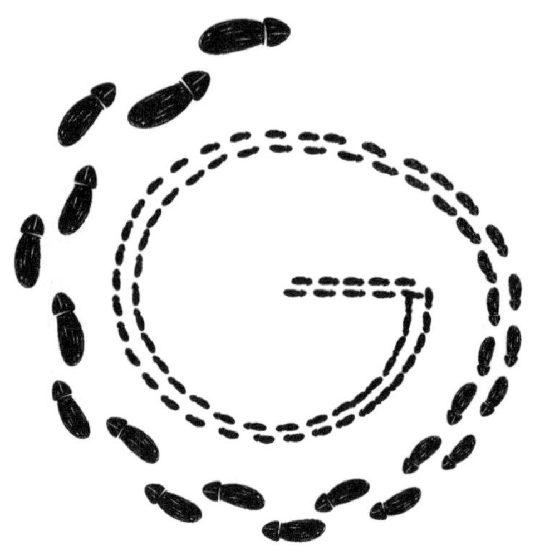

G-Customers: An Investment in Relationships

When you have found your dream customer and have identified who to approach, you must invest in developing a relationship with this individual or group. The customers you are successful with are called your "G-customers". A G-customer is a symbol for the relationship you are forming. G stands for "green", a customer that you are ready to pursue at full speed. In your mind, go around your customer; look at him from different directions. Move closer to him as if you were walking in a spiral. Let the G-customer take the initiative.

Never approach him directly if the customer doesn't show interest. Listen for and act on sales signals. Give the customer the information he needs. This will make it easier for you to get to know one another and the customer will be more open to your reasoning, your opinions and your product.

Many databases differentiate between A, B and C customers. Add G-customer as an additional field. G can also apply in other areas: G-contact, G-person, G-lobbying. A G-customer is a long term investment in relational marketing.

Different industries can use G-contacts for strategic sales when they are faced with big changes. If a company decides to enter an entirely new market, you can begin to influence key people in that new industry to get them to buy the company's values and open doors.

Who do wish to influence? And how?

2
Practical Applications

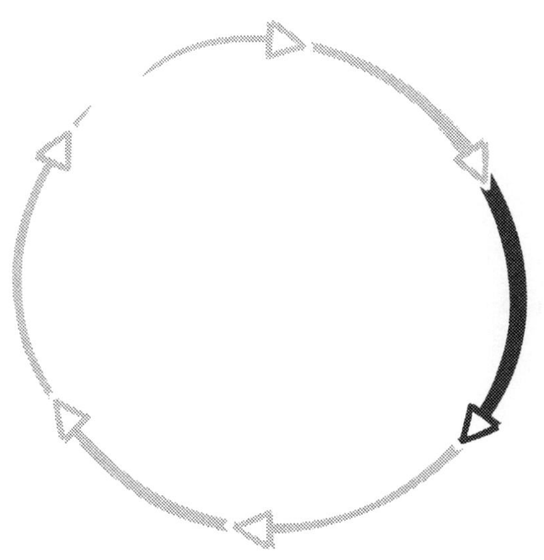

In this chapter, I give a number of examples of both real ad campaigns connected to salespeople and hypothetical cases. Brand names and companies are used for purely educational purposes. Let yourself be inspired to create your own reality and see new opportunities in your organization based on the examples in this book.

Feel free to stand up when you read this chapter. Try lifting one leg and feel yourself losing your balance without falling.

Try to feel yourself losing your footing; it is this imbalance that is the basis for the unexpected. Your body is larger than your brain, so listen to its balance and feel its nuances. Feel the art of losing your balance, yet never falling.

(Note: All the examples are gender-neutral as I make no distinction whatsoever between men and women in skills or opportunities.)

MARKETING AND SALES – THE SALESPERSON AS MARKETING MEDIUM

The problem is often that marketing and sales are two completely separate activities. In the moment of truth – the sales call – there is often no connection to the advertising. In the long-run, many corporations just can't afford it. So what can we do?

Factor 1: Marketing

The connection between advertising and product is often absent at the sale.

Factor 2: Sales

The salesperson is efficient, but expensive without a connection to marketing.

Result Factor 4

Advertising agencies often use different media to get their message out, yet completely forget that the salesperson is also a medium, perhaps the most important of all! The goal is to make every day a kick for the salesperson. If he or she is having fun, their commitment will be forged from iron and motivation will come automatically. The result is that big customers will come to associate the salesperson with variety and entertainment, something that creates long-term business. Entertaining salespeople create extra impact if they act as part of the advertising. The communicative qualities of the advertising can be transferred to the sales force to entertain the customer and inspire the salesperson.

Naturally, the corporate image and the salesperson's credibility must never be jeopardized. A salesperson that knows the business, is not motivated to excellence through sales contests and new sales techniques. What warms a salesperson's heart is the moment of truth, eye to eye with the customer, where sales ability and the merits of the product are tested. It is at this moment that motivation and commitment must be spiced with variety and challenge.

Advertising Lives Longer With the Salesperson As Medium

Naturally, the market's familiarity with a company and its brands makes the salesperson's job easier. As competition for the ear of the consumer increases with today's growing media static, advertising must become more cost-efficient. The salesperson can improve the buyer's recognition of his company by giving him the same added value seen in advertising for the product or give him a live showing of the ad (a meta-product). If the salesperson projects the same feeling as the company's marketing, the buyer will see the bigger picture and will be less sensitive to price.

For a Salesperson, Fun = Success

Show me a buyer who is open and alert when the fifth salesperson of day knocks on the door. The salesperson must have a feel for how much is required to reach the customer through the day's flood of information. People in sales are often talented actors. This image of the salesperson as entertainer can be reinforced by hiring a director to help the sales staff to be more daring. Let common sense set the limits. Choose a salesperson and a customer for a test panel and see how far you can go. This will help you get references and experience that the rest of the sales force can learn from before they go out into the field.

Total Communication Adds Impact

By coordinating information, marketing and sales departments, a company can make a greater impact. Total communication also works as internal marketing for the project. The sales force's enthusiasm will rub off on the marketing department that will in turn motivate the PR department and so on. When different departments work together, it's important to communicate in an easily understood common language.

Entertainment

Many shopping centers have already tried to stand out from the competition by offering their customers entertainment of various types. One shopping center, put on an exhibition called "The King of Rock and Roll", an example of how the market is adopting a more open attitude to what is acceptable. The question is how do the salespeople become "kings" in the eyes of the buyers at a shopping center like this one? Another event is car dealerships that have long arranged Sunday outings for family interested in buying a new car. What happens when the families show up? Sales?

Use your creativity and your imagination and balance them with a well-thought out concept. The following examples are from first-rate advertising campaigns to which I've added my own ideas about creative sales.

The difference between playing and entertaining is skill.

Carlsberg's Salespeople Are Part of the Advertising

Most of us have seen the ad for Carlsberg beer where beer is delivered by a horse-drawn wagon by a bearded Danish man in a distinctive cap. In Denmark, the beer capital of Scandinavia, the ad is often shown live. Salesmen, dressed as the man in the commercial, deliver beer to selected bars and restaurants with a horse-drawn wagon. These salesmen help make the Carlsberg brand more personal and the buyer less price-sensitive. This marketing has increased brand recognition considerably – the man in the commercial is there even when the product is sold. Carlsberg's salespeople are generally more successful than the competition who are not getting as much added value out of their advertising. They lack the same sort of physical connection to their advertising. Carlsberg has created a meta-product.

Through the magnifying glass we can see other successful examples. The car salesman who has the most visible personality is often the most successful. Ice cream trucks melodies create a strong identity and an image. If you don't believe me, change the ringing signal on your cell phone to that of a well-known ice cream truck and see how people around you react.

Other Ways of Connecting Sales to Advertising

OLW Potato Chips Commercial

"Where are the babes?" Everyone in Sweden has seen the commercial: a dozen cool, dark-haired young macho-men in sunglasses stand confidently in a classic bachelor pad, music blasting. One makes a telephone call to a nerdy guy eating a bag of potato chips. "Where are the babes?" the macho man asks. "Are you having a party?" the nerd asks innocently. "Party..." the macho man comments sarcastically to his friends and hangs up. The camera pans out to show the nerd with an apartment full of women literally eating out of his hand.

A great way to get the most out of this commercial would be for the salesperson to ask the head buyer "Where are the chips?" or even to dress like the men in the commercial.

Commercial for Nasal Spray

The print ads for a nasal spray feature a classic black and white picture of Humphrey Bogart with a red clown nose. Here, the salesperson can wear a similar nose when he makes sales calls and encourage the retailer to wear one at the height of the cold season. Playing down the suffering connected with health care products is a challenge with great rewards for those who can find the right balance of humor and credibility.

The PR activities that can be run with the above examples depends on how the different people and departments succeed in working together. (More about this in chapter 6 of this section)

Top of Mind Without Soul Is Wasted Money

Much of the flood of TV advertising by the largest multi-nationals is wasted money. These companies, who are chasing broad target groups have managed to buy top of mind for their brands at an exorbitant price. Many of these products will fail in the long run because they have failed to create a deeper relationship between the consumer and the product. For example, when you move from point A to point B, your buying patterns don't change significantly. Nor do these patterns change when you move product A to market B. Advertising can make you notice a new product, but it isn't until you experience something and buy the product that you go from top-of-mind to the test-of-my-new-consumption-behavior. This is why coordination of sales and marketing is such a powerful force – it reinforces new behavior. Every time you see advertising for the new product, you will relate to an honest experience of the product. Top-of-mind can be compared to first and second gear in a car – it takes a lot of power at the wheels to get a new product rolling. Then, when consumption grows another kind of power is needed to pick up speed. The customer's experiences become part of the actual marketing. Unfortunately, many brands rely on top-of-mind and get stuck in first and second gear, while the customer is expecting to shift into fifth gear. Of course, you can always back up and try again.

This gear shift analogy can also be used to illustrate how sales, marketing, PR, logistics, space management and customer service can work together. Naturally, you can drive in first and second all the time if you are all alone on the road, but there are very few companies who are alone on their markets. The customer can always find something better.

MARKETING – THE PRODUCT IS ITS OWN SPOKESMAN

A simple, yet often forgotten fact is that the product is its own spokesman. The product is the marketing component that comes closest to the target group. All too often, the product development and marketing departments are worlds apart. The product is developed in a relative vacuum, far from the needs of the consumers. Or marketing is completely disassociated from the qualities of the product. When the two departments work together from the beginning to the end, you are more likely to get a product that is taken to heart by the consumer.

Absolut Vodka and the Big Picture

The Swedish brand Absolut Vodka is one of the biggest success stories in the spirits industry. First exported in 1979, Absolut has in record time become one of the best-selling spirits brands in the world. I asked Claes Andréasson of The Absolut Company about their formula for success.

"1: An honest brand with a strong connection to a real product," he answers, "2. A meticulous coordination of advertising, PR, events, image and quality. Our message is a part of everything we do."

"Everyone sees Absolut as an advertising success and image product, but what people forget is behind every powerful image is a powerful story. Our story begins with over 400 years of vodka-making tradition. Every drop of Absolut consumed around the world comes from Åhus, a medieval village in the wheat fields of southern Sweden."

On the surface, it would seem that Absolut's advertising has nothing to do with either Sweden or a Swedish vodka tradition. Yet, how does one explain the cult around the Absolut image? Can an image become part of the popular culture the way Absolut has without being based on strong values. The answer is no. By translating Absolut's quality and history into the correct visual and emotional cues, The Absolut Company has managed to instill these values at a deep visceral level.

"Not everyone knows," Claes Andréasson explains, "that Åhus, Sweden is to Absolut Vodka what Champagne is to champagne and Cognac is to cognac. This is vodka country; home of the very best. What people do know at a very deep level is that Absolut, whatever it is, is a high-quality product that says volumes about the person who is smart enough to consume it. Quality by instinct – that's branding. You just know. From the very beginning we worked methodically to create this relationship to this product. Our ad campaigns are aimed at a narrow segment – trendsetters. Then, these campaigns take a life of their own in the popular mind through well-planned and well-timed PR and events. Contrary to popular belief, most of Absolut Vodka's visibility has been as editorial material in newspapers and magazines and as works of art in museums."

Claes Andréasson is passionate about his product. What sort of passion do you feel for your job? What skills are involved? What does Claes Andréasson have to say about time for creativity?

Thinking Different Makes a Difference

Another company that has managed to make the product its spokesman is Apple Computers. The company's computers replaced the square, gray, box that was once mandatory for all computers with unique modern design and vibrant colors. The computers gave consumers personality and color. Apple's "Think Different" campaign borrows image and personality from the story of Einstein and

Martin Luther King. These people have had a great impact on our history and are a common bond that have brought people closer together. Apple built its Think Different campaign to reinforce their product because it was different.

What would a car built by Apple look like? Why does Apple's advertising address people who already believe in the product more than it does the first-time user? Can a product be superior without succeeding? A case in point: Apple's Macintosh has what many consider a superior operating system, superior hardware, superior design and a brand image that is practically an icon. Yet, Apple has never managed to capture more than 5-10% of the PC market. Why?

The Portrait of the Girl as a Young Bottle

A person that has added a passionate red color to the corporate palette is Richard Branson of the Virgin Company. One of his latest endeavors is the creation of Virgin Drinks headed up by Virgin Cola. The shape of the bottle is modeled after Pamela Anderson who has better curves than Coke.

Which contains more plastic is only a hypothetical question at best. The central issue is how it sells. The use of sex-appeal to sell products is as old as the hills. Often the sex symbols were at a subliminal level; consumer products companies got to be very good at sneaking in a bit of lust. In the case of Virgin Cola, admitting that the bottle is deliberately shaped like Pamela Anderson is a gimmick that is in itself a bit subliminal. (Quick, don't think of pink elephants!)

So what's real? "Fake it until you make it as a brand...then you will become the brand."

The Virgin Company is making use of Detective Marketing principles by observing the market, then challenging it on its own terms. This time it's Coca-Cola that's in for a match. Who will it be next time?

What do you see on the market that's standing still? Like Virgin, anyone can catch the market off-balance. In his book, Richard Branson writes about his fight with the cola giants: "I love giving big companies a run for their money...We thrive on the fact that we are small and a newcomer up against the two giants..." (Branson, 1998).

In other words, big companies make big targets that encourage challengers to go them one better. Big companies can, as in this case, transfer the values of their brand to other arenas. The feelings for a brand attract the buyer to the product, but where do the boundaries for subliminal marketing go?

Do you feel that you have been subliminally influenced to buy a certain product? What are your moral feelings on the subject? Virgin's brand stands for a number of strong feelings that attract the consumer to the product, but how far can they go? When will Virgin create a new planet called the Virgin Planet with balloon tours from England where the president is called Branson. After all, the Virgin Islands feel a little too small for Richard.

Do It Right From the Beginning

In a company, everyone is responsible for a part of the larger picture, yet marketing is often the last link in an uneven chain. What's more, the cost of creating added value after the fact is exorbitant. Working side by side from the beginning saves resources and generates ideas.

Factor 1:

As searching for new opportunities is the basis for my entire method, product development is a natural part of Detective Marketing. Product development without marketing expertise of a product's intangible values (meta-product) contributes to unnecessarily high marketing communication costs.

Factor 2: Marketing

The product has an ability to carry its own added values.

Result Factor 4

A company can adapt its products according to demand.

Below are a number of examples of how to develop products as communicators of added value. There are a few examples where not all of the factors are spelled out. Try defining them for yourself as a learning exercise.

The Floor is Upside Down

Look down at the floor. Can you tell what brand it is? The difference between a name brand and a copy can only be seen on the underside where manufacturers usually put their logos. Off-brand copies are so good today that the name brands' marketing only serves to open the market for the competition. The consumer is only concerned with visible quality, which is often invisible. The floor only has to look like the name brand. For the name brands to survive, they have to go the extra mile to get noticed. The floor company's graphic design can be improved. If the brand is made part of this design, it becomes a more visible part of the product. The brand becomes a spokesman for the product as if the floor were upside down with the logo in plain view. The design of the floor itself is something best left to professionals, but it should be bold and give clear signals as to what floor we're walking on. The goal is to have floor patterns that are a part of the brand and adapted to the target group the company is trying to reach. The right product series can be launched as a whole new category.

"Harsh-Beer"

I return to another beer commercial that features a famous comedian/actor with a hillbilly accent bragging about how he buys "Harsh-Beer" and filters it through a series of tube socks. The commercial is for a medium quality beer which is made with all natural ingredients. The commercial is a comic gem and is just as funny the 15th time around. Yet it has been only a moderate success in creating a strong brand name. The problem: it has created a stronger brand name for "harsh-beer".

Here is a unique opportunity. Why not create a budget brand called Harsh-Beer, sold with tube socks. The teaser could be something along the lines of: "Lose the sissy beer. Harsh-Beer. It's for real. The sock is free."

With its all natural beer, this company is selling a real product by promoting a symbolic one. Actually selling the symbolic one would probably be more profitable. (Note: Since the publication of the original Swedish edition of this book, a Swedish company has applied to register "Harsh-Beer" as a legal trademark. Apparently, I'm not the only one looking for opportunities.)

What opportunities do you see in your market?

Cynical Competition Creates New Demand

NIKE is easily one of the largest sportswear companies in the world. Its distinctive logo, the crooked smile, is a symbol for its aggressive marketing in a high-power world of sports that is a far cry from the basic values these sports were built on. The sports world's cynical elitism is seen more and more often in how track and field and basketball stars are sponsored. The positive social values embodied in sports have been lost in the shuffle. I find it hard to believe that there isn't a growing demand for more human brands in the ordinary sports consumer. Nike has become one of the world's most famous "anti-brands". Nike has left a number of dirty footprints that have created considerable ill-will towards the brand. Read more in *No Logo* (Klein, 2000). When many people unite against a brand, a demand for an alternative is created. Why not develop a straight smile logo, without ulterior motives and cynicism: SMILE Sports. With the right human touch, such a brand could find a large market. Who doesn't want to see kinder Olympic Games, free

from bribery scandals and doping? This brand would be more socially conscious and be associated with sports that not only develop the individual's well-being, but help build a better world as well. A kinder sporting goods brand would open many doors.

The brand owners could be an association of charities. How would your skills come to use in such an organization?

What events should be included in a more human version of the Olympics?

Name three sports personalities that embody SMILE Sport's values.

The Car That Created Added Value

All modern cars look more or less the same. It's strange how the more automotive technology improves, the more anonymous the cars become. It seems as if the only ones buying modern cars these days are technicians, not ordinary people. By putting the magnifying glass on both the product and marketing, we can analyze the situation.

Advertising Background

Factor 1: The Product

Cars are becoming more and more anonymous.

Factor 2: Marketing

It's not the car that is shown; it's the feeling of owning a particular brand that must be conveyed in the advertising.

Factor 4

Ad agencies that market today's anonymous cars don't put much of the car in their commercials. They play to emotions or paint flowers on the product. The car industry's brand vacuum will disappear the day someone does something unusual; for example, if an international mega-celebrity such as Björn Borg starts making cars.

Below is an example that uses Björn Borg, in a purely hypothetical case, as a symbol to emphasize the thoughts behind my fictional scenario. The Bernbach advertising that made the Volkswagen famous in the 60's, was inspired by the product's unique design. We will keep Bernbach in mind as we approach Björn Borg Automotive.

Björn Borg as a Car Brand

This scenario is based on the fact that one can build fantastic media strategies by transferring celebrity to a brand. Brands with personal character have market value. Brands with only technological features lack real value – high technological

standards are today taken for granted. When Björn Borg throws himself into the car business, much of the brand can be built around his celebrity.

The Björn Borg car would be a car-sized tennis ball. The car would not only resemble a tennis ball, but would also be made of a material that resembles that of a ball. Björn Borg would stand for the human touch, security, success, style, sportsmanship, etc. The car's added values would be a bigger selling point than the technical specifications. A car that is a cross between a bug and a tennis ball would be a strong spokesman in itself.

We would read headlines about Björn Borg driving around in a tennis ball. The PR possibilities are limitless.

What parallels and possibilities do you see in your own business?

How would you make a Swatch car a success?

How mobile phones can connect people with more than words

The Finnish company Nokia is a global market leader in mobile phones. They have both strong technical development and are well-connected with other developers around the world. But what about their connection with consumers? Business is evolutionary and when a company has become as successful as Nokia it must take things one step further.

Nokia has spent many years building its brand around the slogan "Connecting people". Early on, they took the lead in user-friendliness and eye-pleasing design. Everything about the brand breathed connectedness in a disconnected world. Today, however, mobile phones are becoming more and more similar and offer more or less the same features. "Connecting people" could just as easily apply to a number of competitors. This is a problem, but also an opportunity.

It is time to take connecting people to the next level and do something to connect them physically as well as theoretically. One way to do this, surprisingly enough, is through hardware design. One solution can be seen below, a new model that can literally bring people together in a new way.

Two mobile phones in one, a sort of mobile yin and yang. (To see it in color go to this book's website.)

It is a known fact that it's always hardest to get people to buy the first product. But what if you when you buy one mobile phone, you get one free. One for yourself and one for a friend. Talk about connection. This not only potentially doubles the number of the company's products out on market, but provides a physical link – the telephone itself.

Here is a prototype of how the new mobile phone could look:

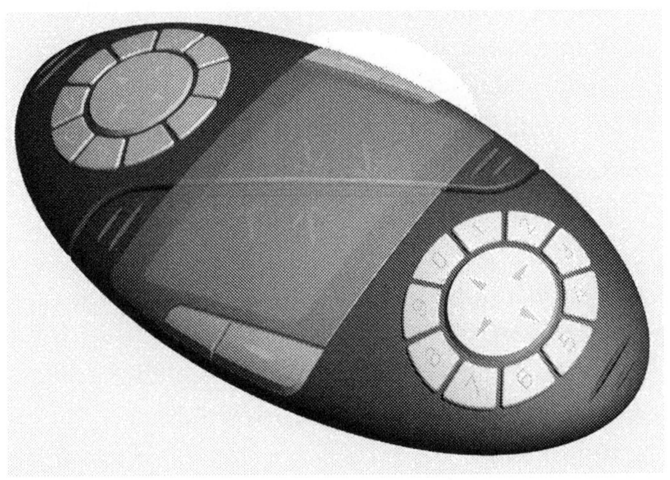

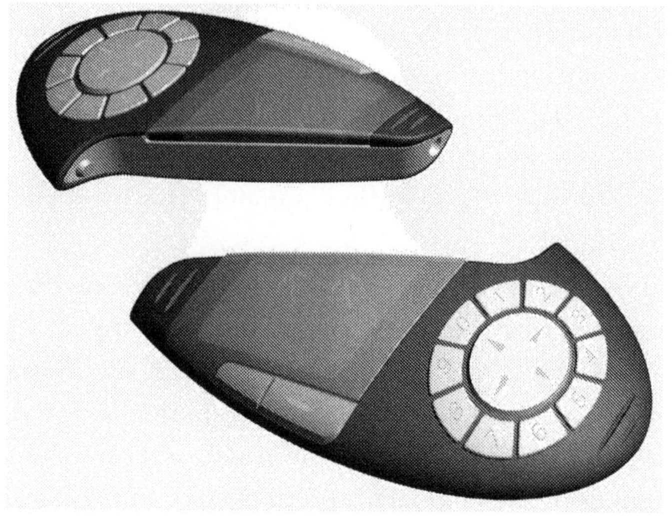

Phone features that connect people

- Magnets hold together the two phones. Two phones become one, two people are brought closer together.
- Free calling to the other person/mobile.
- Special offers and applications at Nokia club.
- Solidarity (sharing batteries and other functions).
- Stereo (impressive sound when the phones are put together).
- Wide-screen picture when put them together.
- Computer connection (sharing Palm functions).

- Games (special versions from leading game brands)
- Pictures (trailers from providers such as Paramount)
- Internet faster with bigger picture (more power)
- Events where you can connect phone with others
- Every sold pair is a small Nokia club
- Special collection of mobile accessories
- Alert sounds when your phone partner is nearby (of/on, practical to use in big cities, large gatherings...and fun too).
- The separate digitals cameras in the phones became high-quality 3D camera.

People need other people. People want to have fun. The Nokia brand can use the technology of their products, the magnet in the phones, as a magnet for people. Nokia could "share the fun" and capture a large share of the "fun market".

There are countless variations on the paired phones theme – matching astrological signs, find a partner theme contests, two player game tournaments – anything that will get people to connect. The key words are buzz and story telling.

What kind of alliances and partnerships could Nokia form to provide content in connecting people? What other products could develop these sort of values through new features and design? With an entire world that badly needs to connect, how can Nokia develop connecting people into social responsibility program (corporate citizenship)? How can a satisfied customer recruit others?

These ideas are only one point of departure for finding ways of getting people to connect with each other.

THE COMPANY – BEING ONE WITH THE BRAND

Be one with the brand instead of number one on the market.

Total communication is built on a simple principle: all drums play together. Companies often forget that the consumer has to have a say. Companies and consumers should find a common set of criteria as a starting point. Internet has shown the importance of taking the consumer's needs into account. Your company can create what the customer wants by identifying needs and building a platform for total interactivity. Keep in mind, companies often grow as a result of customer demands. Companies must begin to let the market into their organization. The customer is interested in the experience of the product or service while the company is focused on the interests of its owners and turning a profit. "The customer is always right" is more true than ever today when the customer can, thanks to the Internet, organize and buy products in bulk at lower prices. "The company is always right when they treat their customers right."

One-to-One stands for a way of thinking with many positive qualities, such as admitting that the customer actually exists. This is the first step towards becoming one with the customer. I would therefore like to take the concept a bit further by renaming it ONE – when two become one, when a company becomes one with the customer. One-to-one creates distance in the form of "us and them", separated by a mental wall. By letting the customer in behind the wall, a sense of community is established. Read more about One-to-One in *The One to One Fieldbook* (Peppers, 1999).

You can see development from mass communication (figure 1) where the same message is broadcast to everyone. The next step takes us closer to the individual's needs (one-to-one) where every relationship is more unique (figure 2). The next mental step is to become one with the market and the customer (figure 3).

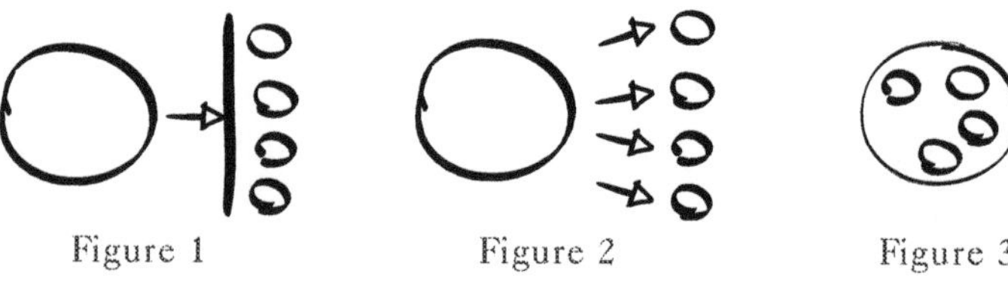

Figure 1 Figure 2 Figure 3

A noticeable development is in the banking world where bank offices have started taking down the Plexiglas and have let the customers' opinions into the organization. The difference is on a deeper level where customers feel the attitude of the salesperson. In interest-based companies, such as mountaineering equipment manufacturers, the board often meets at 7,000 feet above sea level to discuss product development with the top elite of its target group. The Japanese art of war includes frequent references to winning over yourself before winning over anyone else. Perhaps this is the step that is necessary to become one with the market. There is no need to win if you are part of everything else. On the other hand, there is a lot to lose if you lock your company in a box.

ONE – Make the Consumer a Part of the Picture

A successful brand feeds on closeness to the consumer. As companies grow, however, the distance to the consumer also increases. ONE means bringing the customer back into the company. There are many ways of doing this. IKEA, for example, has made the consumer a part of the creative process not only in that he actually assembles the furniture, but also that he can mix and match concepts to create his own look.

"The family that works together stays together" applies to the feeling of closeness that these sort of projects produce. The next step for IKEA could be to involve the consumer in assembling entire showrooms or creating a new collection of completely "do-it-yourself furniture".

This do-it-yourself spirit is two-way. The customer comes to IKEA with a certain openness and meets creations that reinforce his own values. "Why didn't I think of that?" he asks himself when he sees a new piece of furniture or accessory that provides a simple solution to a common problem. IKEA practices what it preaches. It brings the customer into the company.

Everything You Buy is a Longing for Something Else

Buying a product is a yearning for something completely different. This is the basis of all trends. You pay for a tangible object, but you bring home an abstract feeling.

Why do you go to a certain hairdresser? To get your hair cut. This is just as obvious as why people buy from your company. Or is it?

In the beginning of their careers, many hairdressers compete in competitions and try to establish themselves as skillful professionals.

But as they start to build up a clientele they begin to realize that hair is only a small part of what they do. The customer wants to talk about his or her life. My mother, who was a hairdresser for most of her life, tells stories about customers that came for haircuts they didn't need. They didn't mind that most of her cutting was done in the air as long as there was something to talk about. They wanted the social contact. This is a very down-to-earth example of ONE.

What is your company really selling? What could you be selling? How can you use ONE today? Everything on the market is as much an expression of a longing as it is an actual physical object. How can you use this to your advantage?

CNN and ONE

Let's suppose that CNN is, at this very moment, wondering how they can apply ONE to their organization. (Don't worry, I'll let CNN make the final decision themselves. I will, however, with their kind permission, use them as a hypothetical example.)

Today, CNN has over 1 billion viewers. How can the company apply ONE to bring these people into the company? One way is to deepen their relationship with them. Another is to create new relationships between these people. Let's say CNN makes an agreement with Sony to market a CNN Digital News Camera that sends images directly to a web site. People document their own lives and the lives of their friends and neighbors. To allow these people to interact, CNN would create a *ONEcnn.com* with free homepages for everyone who has purchased a starter kit. This site would not only supply news from country to country, but also from community to community, family to family and even individual to individual. This news would in no way compete with existing news coverage, but rather complement it just as the local press does today. Over the years, we have seen the power of the small community newspaper as a marketing medium. Somewhere along the line, these one billion people will turn into consumers, with CNN first in line to turn their needs into revenue.

CNN already uses much journalistic material from viewers who happened to be on the spot when news broke. With one billion relationships, there will be far more on-the-spot reporters. This would also create a stronger relationship between sender and receiver when they are ONE.

Picture being ONE-line live with one billion people where you chose the camera or the film. "Honey, could you give me the remote control so I can change camera angles."

What can one billion customers do for CNN or your company?

Napster and ONE

Legal or illegal, the success of Napster's on-line community of music lovers shows the power of ONE. Napster's one-to-one file sharing has established a sort of global library of music accessible to everyone. If we look beyond the copyright issues, this is an example of letting the customer be a large part of the business idea.

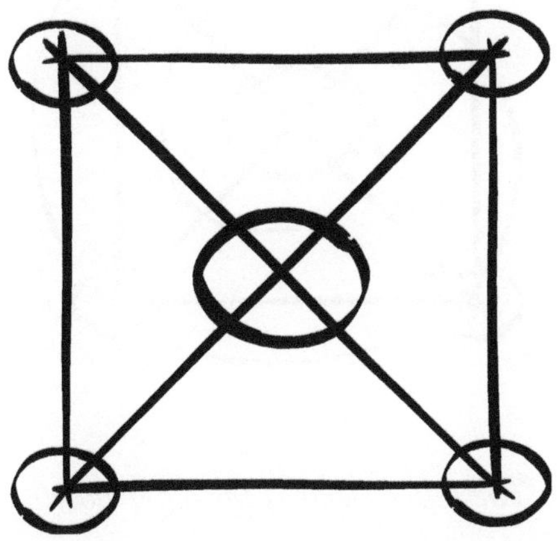

Illustration: A company's customers form a relationship to the company where the company is no longer essential.

Napster's approach turns enthusiasm into a way of running a company. What's more, the act of consuming itself becomes a strong part of the entertainment.

If Napster fails to run its company, the consumers will run it for them through the organic channels they have developed in using the service.

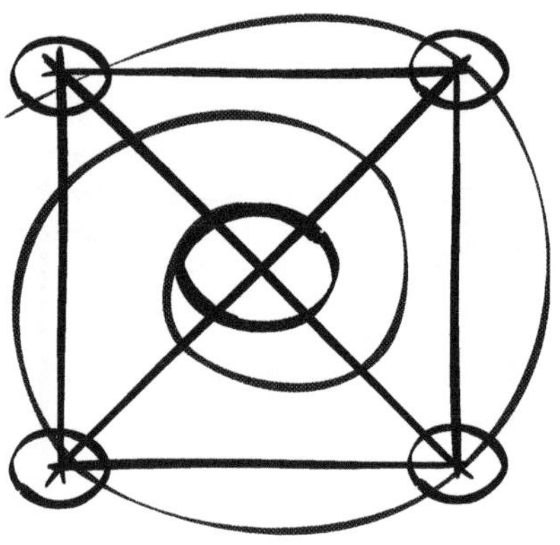

Illustration: The inner circle is the outer border of ONE. The outer circle is the company's outer sphere and the smaller circles are the customers. The arrows symbolize borders that are moving out so that the company can grow with the new world.

Some companies have more customers than the population of small countries. Letting the customer into the company is a way of utilizing this power. In a changing world, where both literal and figurative borders are constantly changing, a new world order is slowly taking form. ONE creates new borders by moving the existing borders to the company ever further out from the company.

At its core, ONE is self-perpetuating. Focus on the idea that set the process in motion. What components keep the company rolling forward? Does its processes have a soul, a deeper meaning? If the soul is missing, there is a risk that employees have forgotten the core of ONE: the customer. Today, customers sometimes know more than the company representatives that serve them. Why not use this know-how and enthusiasm to teach employees to follow rather than lead.

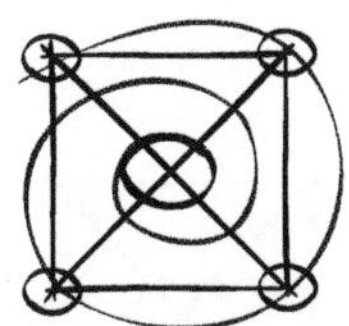

The illustration above shows complete interactivity between all parties. The energy continues both outside the process and moves inwards so that energy can flow freely in this self-perpetuating process.

How 2 Million Car Buyers Can Get a Better Deal

A car is like milk: it can be produced just about anywhere. The difference between different cars is the degree to which they are perfected. One approach is to manufacture your own car using a website. Think of a manufacturer that gets parts from his suppliers and design from his customers. When the customers drive away from the factory in their new cars a community is formed. With no advertising, you have created a no-brand car with 2 million owners.

Companies must realize that the customer truly is king when many customers converge at the same place on the Internet. Instead of engaging in "brand wars", companies should involve the customer in their daily business. Companies that act cynically, will discover that the wrath of the king – the customer. Their brand can easily become a symbol, an anti-brand.

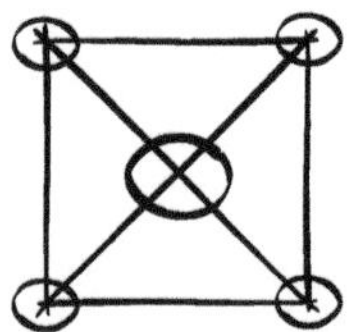

Customers around a company organize themselves in such a way that the company is no longer necessary.

Napster is an example of the power of ONE. How is it being used?

All too often, corporate communications are focused on the company itself. Customers find it difficult to get involved when they see no connection to their own situation. Hollywood is a wonderful place for creativity, but if too many films are about Hollywood, creativity will suffer. In the corporate world, the audience must feel that they are part of things. If both the customer and the company don't both get noticed, they don't exist.

One of Sweden's biggest international success stories is the furniture company IKEA. IKEA could, using the Napster model, develop its business even further. By creating a site where people could buy, sell and trade their IKEA furniture, profitability could be extended to include the entire lifetime of the products. Furniture bought on this collective site could be picked up at a "shareroom" at the nearest IKEA store. The customer drops off and picks up his furniture himself, minimizing logistics. IKEA would charge a small commission on each sale. The buyers of new and used furniture meet and consumption of new furniture would increase in the long run as a community is created. Statistics from the sales of used furniture would be invaluable research material and a way of staying on top of developing trends –

when a new wave of 70's nostalgia hits, it will be noticeable first in the used market. The same with trends in color, fabrics, etc.

The PR potential is also interesting. Maybe that used sofa you're buying once belonged to a celebrity. What other opportunities do you see? Can IKEA offer customers a better price for products that will stay within the IKEA sphere? Can this idea be applied to the auto industry? Are there environmental benefits? How would it feel to see your furniture in the home of a friend's house or that of a complete stranger?

How much is 17% of IKEA's product over the past five years? What is the revenue potential of commissions on that sum? Perhaps, these sales will stimulate car sales as some people decide to buy bigger cars and other products as a result of this new behavior. How does this affect profitability?

The Late Show, with David Letterman, is more than entertainment; it's an historic milestone. Much of the show's success is built on the fact that its content is created by the audience. David uses the studio audience and the general public to create moments of superb comedy and satire. Here again, is an example of ONE. The audience is given a face and the viewer at home feels that he is participating in the show. This phenomenon illustrates the need for confirmation in interactive meetings between senders and receivers. *"How many would use a mirror if they couldn't see themselves?"*

E-Commerce with ONE

IT has taken us away from much of the classic B-to-B and B-to-C marketing and given us C-to-C: Computer to Computer. There is an unwillingness to recognize the target as an individual person; the individual is complex and hard to control. The goal in working towards ONE is to add interaction to entertainment to turn the customer into the advertisement. Once the adage for the corporate world was: "If no one has heard of your company, you don't exist." Today, for those working towards ONE the saying becomes: "If no one has heard of your company and your customers, you don't exist."

The relationship between many e-commerce companies and their customers looks something like this: [FirstName] [LastName] [@] [Address] [City] – a relic from direct advertising transferred to the web. Creating communication platforms for all the different market segments within the target group requires a bit of work, but can be worth it. At Letsbuyit.com, we increased sales 30% after putting together such a platform. The lesson is that those who move forward methodically using analysis, tests and evaluation can often find new paths to success.

Many banks have been encouraging their customers to use their Internet services by offering a number of discounts and benefits. This carrot on a stick approach has shortened the learning curve and helped customers accept the new way of banking. The new sites add an extra dimension of direct marketing to very specifically-defined target groups. Read more about online community in *Release 2.1* (Dyson, 2001).

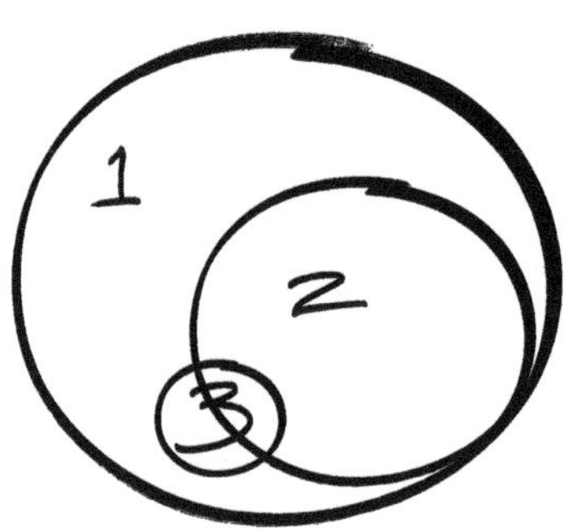

Customer Behavior

1. Not comfortable with the net as a place to do business. Expensive to attract as customers.

2. Pay their bills via the Internet.

3. Buy on credit via the Internet.

Banks and e-commerce can work together to reach ONE by creating positive synergies. The bank can help establish contact with customers and between the customers, while the e-commerce company can help banks get closer to their customers with custom-tailored offers, letters, advertising, etc. Special offers can be especially attractive since credibility has already been established and the threshold to buying is lower than it would otherwise be. Consumer behavior is determined to a large extent by seasons, holidays and pay-days. I call this *"time to cash in"*.

When does your company have its "time to cash in" and what factors are at work?

A Few E-Things to Keep in Mind

Applying ONE to e-commerce means keeping a few things in mind.

- Remember, community is invisible. Your members cannot see each other. Encourage interaction.
- If your employees are too invisible you create an ATM feeling towards the customer. If the customer has a feeling of personal contact, the customer's problems can be a positive source of growth.
- Just as employees have hidden talents, so do the customers.

- Changing behavior and buying patterns takes time. Being original puts you ahead in the long run if it reinforces the feeling of ONE.
- Taking care of suppliers is just as important as taking care of customers.
- Create synergy in everything you do. If you sell a TV, that customer should be put on DM lists for video offers, etc.
- Learn from the gaming industry: publicize your winners.
- Be first in creating product trends and get the message out with the appropriate PR.
- Be very clear about who you are. Support charities whole-heartedly. Have a mission. A good example is Patagonia, a company that practices what it preaches.
- Your site should be at least 50% information or entertainment. The principle is the same as putting the milk at the back of the store: the customer comes to you for one thing, but ends up buying a few other things he didn't realize he needed.
- It is important to give people a story to tell. Every product or service should come with a story.
- Internet is an evolving new society with its own values, where the customer is always king. How is your company treating "the king"?

- We need more jazz in e-commerce. Everyone should get a chance to play a solo, but the important thing is how you play together and how you play to the audience. It comes down to touching people and putting a little meaning into their lives. Street musicians get next to their customers without paying rent. You'll find street musicians where their customers are, yet these musicians don't live on the money they get, but rather on the music they play. How can you jam with your customers? The interface of e-commerce with traditional stores, when old meets new, can result in wonderful music.
- Many times it seems as if active, enthusiastic customers are discouraged. This happens when a company has an unrealistic perspective of how interesting they are to me as a customer. I call this *Overkill Marketing* – marketing something so aggressively that you kill the customer's enthusiasm. Sound familiar?

Where Did the Little Satisfied Customer Go?

Dissatisfied customers are always seen and heard. The satisfied ones tend to be less vocal. Getting satisfied customers to be active is the first step towards creating a community. Many companies are good at building up customer complaints departments, but less so at devoting resources to harnessing the positive energy of the satisfied customer. Can you tell which the five most satisfied costumers are for your company?

All companies, e-commerce companies in particular, must make the most out of every customer "story". Stories sell products and build image. Create your own dynamic target group; give your customers a chance to see each other. For example, if you've sold 3,000 digital cameras, why not organize an online photo competition? If you've sold 3,000 scooters, why not organize an off-beat scooter event in the local park (covered by the media). Or, less spectacular, but very effective, is a regular e-mail newsletter with tips, advice and letters from readers / customers. *"Customers love customers, but who loves your company?"*

I call this search for contact with the customer *members' voices*. Sometimes members' voices can simply not be heard. Banks and e-commerce companies often receive e-mail and correspondence by the hundreds of thousands. Members' voices often end up as echoes in the wastepaper basket. Long-term success means that two-way communication is a high priority. If the companies themselves don't make the most of their members' voices, someone else will. Other companies will see the opportunity and make the most of it.

Today's customer contact often ends with a deep echo in a wastepaper basket because the company cannot deal with individuals on a large scale. These wastepaper baskets are full of gold for those who know how to let customers take care of each other. It is in here you will find the strength of members' voices. There are many ways of doing this. In certain companies, I have seen a 20% increase in sales using members' voices. One example of the power of this idea is the Sidney 2000 Olympics. Participation creates enthusiasm, in this case as 46,000 volunteers. The TV audience was estimated at 3.5 billion. We all heard the song "We will be ONE." For the closing ceremonies, all participants entered the arena without being divided into nations. This can be compared with the corporate world when companies and their customers can walk together. People are the least utilized resource in today's corporate world. How can this be changed?

How did the 46,000 volunteers affect the 3.5 billion TV viewers? What is the nature of a similar constellation at your company or at a company where you are a customer?

ONE can also be a system to build something together where the definitions of who does what are fluid in nature. An example is X Island, "the holiday

Island". When I was on X Island last summer, I met guests that had been coming there since the beginning of the 70's. Some of these regulars had literally built the place together with those that ran it. We lived in huts, did the dishes, cleaned and cooked together with the staff, all in 100° heat. That customers who had actually paid for the privilege of building the compound made the stay very interesting. Remember: shared experience is an excellent way of strengthening the product.

Take your insurance company, for example. How many floors of their office building could you as customer have had a hand in building? How would this have affected your relationship? The company merely initiates the customer stairway; it is the customer that turns it into an escalator. When customers learn from each other, a self-perpetuating process is created.

On X Island, some 80% of the participants had come based on word of mouth. This process could be reinforced. If, for example, you were to give all 60 participants 20 printed postcards with postage, the message would spread so much faster. When the cards were mailed, approximately 1,200 friends would have learned of a great experience.

You could also post 60 pictures of the participants on the net so that their friends could share their experiences as they booked their own stays. These sort of transparent customer systems are very self-perpetuating when customers see themselves and are a part of the value of the service. If you run a restaurant you need a good chef and guests who tell friends who enjoy that sort of food. My advice is to skip the ads and concentrate on hiring better chefs. Unfortunately, many companies don't start with the goods or services that they are selling. In the case of the good restaurant in my example, they did. I now eat there and have told all my friends. Read more about this in *Unleashing the Idea Virus* (Godin, 2000).

Dress Code According to ONE

Dressing like the customer makes it easier to be accepted by that target group. Clothes, tattoos, piercing, slang and behavior should all be based on the employee's interests. A company that utilizes this principle is Universal Music, where people dress like the fans of the music they work with – hard rockers, Barry White fans, Elton John fans, etc) This makes them more credible in stores, at concerts and with customers. Every person at the office has his or her own stereo. Taste can not be dictated by a hierarchy. "The Management's Greatest Hits Collection" would probably not be a hit. To achieve ONE, you must see things through the customer's eyes and be part of his world. The difference between ONE and cheap opportunism comes down to genuineness.

The saying "Don't judge a man until you've walked a mile in his shoes" should be changed to "Walk a hundred miles in the customer's shoes if you want to sell him a new pair of shoes."

There is nothing wrong with outsourcing. Yet, the customer can act as "insourcing" at the heart of the company. Sometimes, companies hang the horse in front of the carrot. The customer needs no carrot as long there is someone at the company who listens. Explain.

Have you ever felt that you were ONE with the company you are presently doing business with? Have you ever had business transactions that were made with the heart as well as with the wallet?

What does ONE mean in your work – in product development, communications, etc.?

What pros and cons do you see in the ONE concept?

What doors have been opened? How has it affected your business?

Bill Gates is important for Microsoft, but the users are more important in the software Linux. Describe how Linux work with the power of ONE.

What is it that drive the buyers at eBay.com? Or is it the buyers that drives eBay? Describe how they work with ONE.

The Visible Service Portfolio – How to Milk Cows in a City Park

One way of making your portfolio of services tangible is to build some sort of showroom. Whatever you call it, it is a way of conceptually consolidating all your attractive values, making your company's values visible. Success is based on total interactivity between the visitor and the exhibitor, where the visitor is treated to a sample of your services in a very concrete way.

A local dairy products company has long had a stylized cow as a familiar symbol. Today, however, the connection between a cow in a barn and milk in a carton isn't as emotionally clear as it once was. Most children grow up in cities where cows are rare pets. Nor are summer vacations spent in the country. They are many people who have never seen a real cow and have no emotional response to the connection between the product and the source. Why not turn a entire city park into a large farm where children can see first hand where cows live, how they are milked and the connection between the animal – the cow – and the product – milk. A showroom in the same spirit can reassure people who are concerned about what goes into their food in these times of genetic engineering and functional foods and give them more information about the product. A park showroom can be an eco-farm, an active forum for discussions about food and a meeting place for farmers from around the country – a place for good 'ol common sense.

Reflection: Communication often creates side effects. Perhaps urban dwellers will start wearing checkered shirts and boots. The be-yourself- look can be promoted. "Come and milk your own cow in the park! Make your own cheese, churn your own butter!"

What other communication opportunities do you see? And what about effects on exports? Training of retailers? Connections to grocery store loyalty cards? Are there quality issues?

How can you make your business tangible?

Ask people around you; they may see values that you've missed.

The dumbest question is the one you never asked and the answer you never got. There are no dumb questions, only an on-going search process.

Showroom Naturelle

A similar example is products that are connected with the great outdoors. The relationship is not always visible in the city, nor are the activities of environmental groups tangible. It is only when there is a concrete connection to what these groups are trying to protect, that a genuine response and true commitment can be inspired. Manufacturers of sporting goods, outdoor clothing, fishing equipment, jeeps and the like have a strong need to communicate on a concrete level. Even nature reserves and national forests can be marketing in a more tangible way. A showroom can be built at a subway station or an airport. The showroom could feature a real forest with live animals and a babbling brook. Climate and genuine forest sounds can be simulated in realistic manner. From the subway with fluorescent lighting straight into the woods. There can be "moose crossing" signs posted around town along with teasers reading: "Deer have been sighted in the subway!" When the country literally comes to the city, more big city people will become aware of the importance of a clean environment.

The total market for all participating companies would increase proportional to the amount of increased environmental consciousness. Environmental groups can communicate that this is something we all must work together to solve. The target group is active people, that is, people in motion and these people are most easily reached in a subway or at the airport. Where there is movement, there is also consciousness. When consciousness is affected new forms of communications are created.

Experiences in showrooms show conscious or sub-conscious needs which lead to new patterns of consumption.

Other countries' tourist boards could use showrooms in subways to build miniature replicas of their respective countries. One week Turkey, the next, Tanzania. The idea is to wake curiosity and a longing to see the country for oneself. What values are created when the subway company can advertise: "We can take you around the world, one flight down"?

I leave it to the reader to ponder the implications.

Message, Results and the Advertising Mid-Wife

Factor 1: Message

The race for results means the advertising message and design have become increasingly provocative to be heard.

Factor 2: Results

If ad campaigns are not highly profitable, companies can buckle under from the astronomical marketing costs involved.

Effect Factor 4

By taking not just market share, but also creating a market, a company creates room to grow.

WARNING! The following example is somewhat cynical and was created with no consideration for the sensitive nature of the subject it concerns.
I ask the reader to bear with me.

When is Advertising a Mid-Wife?

On extremely competitive markets advertising often doesn't pay. This leads to companies staking out new markets. Diaper manufacturers today find themselves in such a situation. The market is flooded with products and improved ways of keeping your baby's bottom dry. Let's try a fictional example using Pampers.

Suppose Pampers wants to find a new market. They buy 100,000 addresses to couples who have been married or living together for three years in a given area. If Pampers can encourage these couples to have children within a year, their market will grow considerably. With a response rate of 3%, this would mean 3,000 new customers that use 6 diapers per day for a total of 700,000 more diapers sold in a year.

In this case, the cost of the campaign is now easily paid for by increased sales. Once a database with 6,000 new customers has been created, other products can be marketed in the same way or the names can be sold to makers of strollers, baby food, car dealerships, etc. Sales to other retailers alone would pay for the entire campaign.

All moral issues aside, the example serves to illustrate the opportunities for creating a new market.

The battle to create a market and capture the consumer first has intensified lately along with issues of privacy. One way of actively searching for birthrate trends is using the Internet. The Baby Basics site, for example, deals with the final months of pregnancy. Here visitors are encouraged to send electronic postcards to pregnant friends to encourage them to introduce their newborn to joys of consuming as early as possible. The friend receives a starter kit up to 8 weeks before the baby is due. By the time she wakes up in the maternity ward, the baby has already gotten his first advertising message.

MARKETING – PR AND INFORMATION

Corporate communications depend on how the company respects and integrates its different resources. The marketing department doesn't always work well with the PR and corporate communications departments. One reason is that budget and accounting work are often more important than the larger picture. There is a considerable lack of understanding for the idea of overall market communication.

Good teamwork between marketing and PR departments often goes unnoticed. Advertising is visible, but its interplay with editorial material is less so. Sometimes this interplay is most noticeable when it is missing.

Corporate communications should always be taken into account when planning for the long term. It is only then that communication can have its full effect. PR and information give a company's image credibility. Success depends on how well your company succeeds in coordinating its efforts.

The market for communication is growing along with the number of new companies and networks. Their solutions are built on both local and global teamwork. Even the border between customer and supplier is getting blurry. Work today is more result-oriented. Teamwork between the marketing and PR departments can be improved using internal communication networks. These networks can act as a forum where everyone can exchange experiences to create flexibility, a larger perspective and a better view of the big picture.

Discuss teamwork.

Discuss a couple of ad campaigns and how they can be reinforced with the right PR. What effects will this have? How can you strengthen the corporate image by learning to work together with other departments?

What trends can you identify around you? What are you doing to make the most of them? How can you affect them?

See your work as an informal tango. Let the result carry you to your goal. Use simple language, seek the proper imbalance.

COMPANIES AND CHARITY – VALUES ARE GOOD PRODUCT PLACEMENT

Man's eternal conflict between good and evil is as timely as ever. The media's instant coverage of far away events has created a global consciousness and a global conscience. Blessed are the humble, for they have great buying power. We saw this when environmentalism came to stay. There is a market for doing good.

"It is only when evil kisses good that a new world can be created. Evil contains power and know-how. If every bullet fired in the former Yugoslavia had been a seed, the region would have been a rainforest to stroll in, instead of a mass grave to cry over."

Before, it was countries who had the power to change the world. Today, much of the power and resources are in the hands of the world's large corporations. The corporate world is evolving and changing shape to meet the demands of the market. "Evolution" has become the eternal free market, something that we would all like to control, but which actually controls us, for better or worse.

The corporate world not only has the resources to change or save the world, they can transform it into a warm heart in a cold universe. When corporations contribute to making the world more human, we are brought closer to one another as part of the bigger picture, a sort of yin and yang of earth.

Companies that work with good intentions often do so quietly, developing hidden talents in the process. Their know-how and experience could serve as a model for other companies. Perhaps showing one's soft side is still considered a weakness in the corporate world. But undervaluing good, gives evil more power. We need a pragmatic form of education in the subject for both schools and the corporate world. Maybe there's room for a sort of stock exchange of goodness alongside the traditional one for paper. There, values could grow along with profits on shares. Companies should start making the connection between this moral capital and the dedication of its employees part of its accounting. This is an important profitability variable.

I call this "management by goodness". This idea is not based on the traditional picture of companies donating to charitable organizations. It is based on the view that the corporate world sees its business as a part of the evolution of the earth. Goodness should be seen as a natural part of business and should be accounted for as spiritual profits.

Here are some questions that can serve as food for thought. (Note: answers cannot be found at the back of this or any other book.)

Why are we here? Where do we fit into the big picture? What values are we contributing to society / the earth? We are not God and He is not on the board directors, so what can we do ? There is more spiritual profit in helping countries that have major problems than investing in countries with exploitable riches such as oil. Who wants to be a mentor for the survival of the universe?

The realization that corporations can operate more humanly is growing and the number of companies taking it to heart is increasing. Mutual funds that only make "moral" investments have appeared as a guiding star for the good corporate citizen. One of many examples is KPA's Ethical Mutual Funds (Sweden). The funds are marketed as the ethical choice in the battle between good and evil. KPA's slogan is "Good returns with a clean conscience." The funds are selling well, even though we're more interested in the company's values than in the actual make-up of its portfolio. Nevertheless, other mutual funds are following suit.

Product Placement of Values

Corporate communications can include goodness as part of its message. In today's youth culture, for example, strong brands influence values more than ever. These companies sell more than products and services; they sell human values. Companies that sell detergent, food and the like are very profit-oriented. They can see the connection between PR and good image and how it can affect sales. Their goals, in a way, overlap those of charitable organizations. Charities can approach these corporations in much the same way as many companies approach Hollywood for product placement. They can convince these companies to "place" values in their advertising, making it possible for charities to get their message out at a reasonable price. Credibility can be balanced by the right relationship between the message and the brand. One example is a diaper manufacturer that often uses endearing babies in its communications. Since children are the future inhabitants of the earth, there should be a deeper meaning to the message. With the incredible amount of advertising we produce, this sort of advertising would come as a breath of fresh air in our consumer society. Perhaps we could make the message the medium by creating a new category in various advertising awards honoring "the promotion of human values in advertising". A prize of this kind would also increase advertising's credibility in general and counter the cynicism that makes consumers turn a deaf ear to advertising messages.

When sponsoring, one should not use criteria such as "value for money", but rather "value for mind"; that is, what sort of reactions does the sponsoring evoke for the company, both internally and externally. Or, simple how it feels to do a good deed.

One way of working with good values is to limit the exposure given to bad values. An anti-smoking lobby group, Non-Smoking Generation, works with an ad agency to influence the values that its ads promote. For example, are smokers romanticized in advertising directed at young people? This can be a very effective way of building a base of good values through good communication. Other organizations could use similar approaches to affect the content of advertising in a positive way.

Naturally, no one wants advertising to be an educational enterprise. The crux is what you want to sell and how far you are willing to go to get your message out. As always, common sense is an important ingredient in finding the right balance.

Microsoft
PlayStation
ABSOLUT
VODKA
Carlsberg
ROLEX
SAS
McDonald's
ABB
NIKE
Reebok

A BRAND

NEW WORLD

Coca-Cola
I vårt hem
"Glöm inte Coca-Cola!"

Game, set…

BORG
... match Borg.

HARSH–BEER. IT'S FOR REAL.

(THE SOCK IS FREE.)

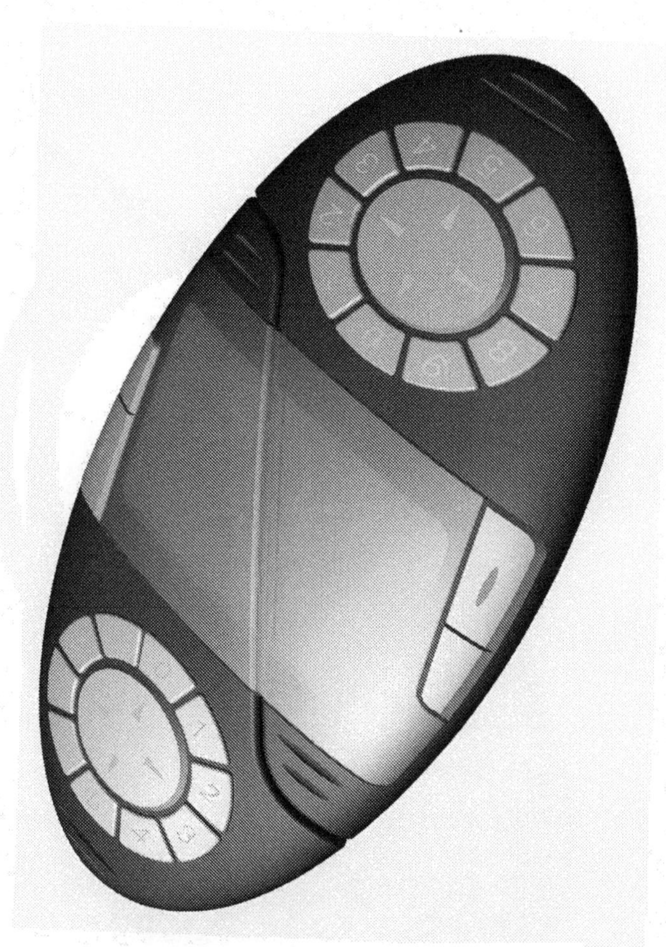

NOKIA
Connecting People

NOKIA
Connecting People

3
Creative Communication

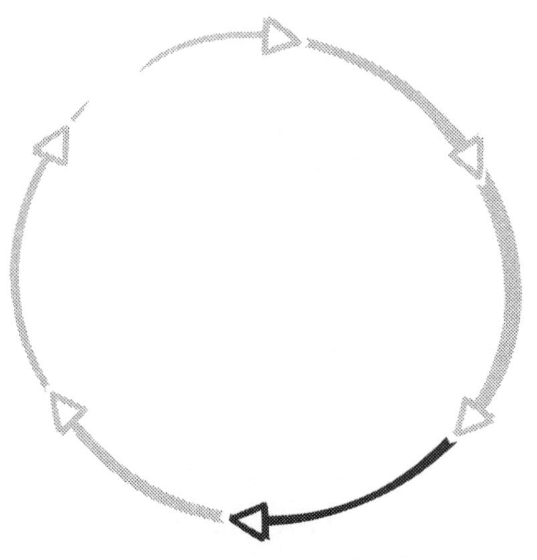

A key ingredient in creating strong brands is creative communication. In this chapter, we'll take an uncomplicated look at this form of creativity. Common sense combined with expert marketing know-how can go a long way.

Innovative web agencies have finished playing around and are starting to merge with large consulting companies. The result is a larger portfolio of services and a new level of expertise. A similar merging of advertising agencies and management consultants could be another potential development.

If we compare the sum total of all marketing know-how to a chess board, ad agencies would be square C-4. Playing chess and winning, however, means that you have to do more than take care of your own little square. You must have a broader perspective and think strategically. Why not use teamwork and play using all the squares? The courage to meet, adds new dimensions in many different areas.

Interest in advertising and media effectiveness has been increased over the years by events such as the Effies, The Advertising Effectiveness Awards.

Campaigns such as those by Benetton have stretched the boundaries for what we will tolerate and what advertising should/can contain.

Provocativeness gives advertising's C-4 a larger field in which to communicate.

Psychology and behavioral science are important elements in all communication. The goal of all advertising is to get the customer to see his need for a product or service as essential. This kind of know-how is hard to define and can best be described as intuition.

A theory by Aleksej Leontiev (1902-1979) reasons that psychological needs are more important than physical ones. This means that the hunger for the "right" brand can take precedent over physical hunger. In American youth culture, the behavior is very apparent in neighborhoods where teenagers feel that having seven pairs of basketball shoes of the right brand is more important than food for the day. This is a sad situation, but there is hope: those companies that become successful through social conscience.

My interpretation of the problems in much of today's marketing is summarized by a simple adage: If you plant rice you harvest rice; you can't sit around waiting for tomatoes.

CREATING SYMBOLIC BRANDS

When Coca-Cola was introduced in Sweden in the 1950's, the company deliberately placed its product in a symbolic context. An early example is the illustration in the ad "A table at a country parsonage". The illustration showed a home where everything was proper and traditional.

At that time, many feared that America's rock and roll culture would undermine Sweden's characteristic tranquility. The 1954 illustration by Ib Thanings associated the "dangerous" soft drink with traditional home values and the brand was welcomed with open arms.

Historical brands such as Coca-Cola would be extremely expensive to create today. The wall of information and consumption is bigger than ever, creating a need for symbolic acceptance in the consumer. Advertising must play on emotions that the consumer is familiar with from an earlier context. Recognition must be borrowed from other familiar symbols. The automotive industry is full of symbolic brands. The Jaguar is a symbol for natural strength and elegance. Ferrari has a spirited horse standing on its rear legs. The horse symbolizes movement and power. Other industries use a number of symbols to define their business. The more obvious examples are a restaurant with a fork and knife and a beauty salon with a pair of scissors. The goal is immediate recognition.

The Swedish bank Föreningssparbanken has a well-known brand that is embodied in a large metal coin hanging in front of its offices. The coin, however, contains "inauthentic" symbolic values since it has no monetary value. To utilize the symbolism of its brand, the bank should issue a real coin and send it to the entire population of the country. This would give the brand a physical, concrete foundation. What brands do feel embody meaningful symbolism?

Another development in the symbolism's role in advertising is the association of natural values with man's green conscience.

A brand's symbolic language can be enriched by "sponsoring the environment". This can give a company a good reputation and can encourage journalists to write about Ferrari's work with horses, Jaguar's work with jaguars and so on. Push and pull. A company's good will is always in question. What is Ferrari doing to save the wild horses? After all, what company wants to have an extinct brand? This is one way of using the market to make a positive contribution to the environment.

Those companies that use a logo that resembles a globe – what are they doing to help the planet? "Global business relies on a global world." Multinationals are facing increasing opposition from consumers as they become symbols for the world in which we live. This means that no matter how cynical a company may be, they must take the customer's opinions and wallet into consideration in our information age.

"The Rhino is not an endangered Species" reads the provocative teaser in this ad for WWF.

This kind of thinking opens new doors for your company. Even if my examples may sound a bit unlikely, it is ultimately the market that decides.

A Slightly More Personal Example – The Personals

A personal ad is a very interesting piece of communication, one that we're all familiar with. The one who places the ad – the sender – describes himself as "he would like to be", rather than "what he is really like". Based on this, he seeks someone who answers the description of "what he wants" rather than "what he needs." From these four parameters, the reader – the receiver – reads "what he wants" rather than "what he needs." Then these two people meet, with red carnations worn like product logos to make them stand out from the gray masses.

This can be translated to the corporate world where many brands are "wanna-brands" that are one thing in their advertising, but another in real life. Almost all advertising is read like the personals, especially want ads. This is based on the idea that the customer must have this sort of picture to buy what he already needs. I call this stage "fake it 'till you make it branding". Wouldn't it be easier to just wear a red carnation and say "Here I am."

This is one reason that reference marketing is growing in homes where Tupperware and the like are being sold from friend to friend. I call this face to face. People love people. Who wants a hidden agenda?

What products have you bought by recommendation from a friend?

Certain companies claim that the difference between their advertising and reality is that they wish to change their reality. What does this mean?

TEMPORARY ADDED VALUES

Variety and Acknowledgement

"When was the last time you brought your wife flowers?". The slogan is a familiar one in advertising. Marriage is built on a combination of variety and acknowledgement. When was the last time you gave your customer flowers – *when did you last acknowledge your relationship with him or her?* A limited number of products can create variety for big consumers that, for example, "eat at home with McDonald's."

The Added Values of the Seasons Create Demand

It is obvious that certain products have a natural relationship with our four best marketers: the four seasons. Surprisingly many products can be associated with the needs of the changing seasons. For example, the chain of opticians with its late spring campaign: "Buy contact lenses today, get a pair of sunglasses free." Contact lenses symbolize mobility and an active lifestyle while sunglasses in this case show the optician's concern for his customer. This unique combination leads to the right buying decision. Timing is important and the right media planning essential. Since the seasons always return and are an incentive to consumption they can be part of a company's long-term planning.

Another example of seasonal and climactic buying is my computer and the free bicycle that came with it. When the first warmth of spring clears the snow from the ground, who doesn't feel a longing for a new mountain bike? Macintosh is the name of the computer that I write on when I'm not riding my bike. The connection between the two products for me, as for many others, was that I needed both products at the same time.

Trends and events can result in added value when there is a direct connection to the product. Total communication, however, often ends right after the purchase. Seeing the bigger picture together with a bit of entertainment will give a product a longer life. When do customers become a part of the Ericsson brand and part of its total interactivity? Event marketing seldom activates the consumer to take action. Ericsson has invested heavily in product placement in the James Bond film "Tomorrow

Never Dies". By creating an entire series of Bond products, the company is creating added value (a metaproduct). The strategy should be taken one step further: the audience should be given a part in the film. The customer can activate a number of Bond functions. The phone must feature games and entertainment. Sometimes the customer receives messages in his phone "You have been chosen for a secret mission. Go to the Ericsson store on Main Street" where you will be given more information. When the customer comes to the store, he is treated to activities with other agents, given up-dates, etc. When the customer becomes James Bond, he becomes a salesman for the product... as long as he doesn't try steering his car with the phone.

When can we expect to see a woman as Bond; or will she be called Bondi? And who would play the part? What products can be marketed? *How would this affect the selection of products for women?*

A meeting of Ericsson and Alta Vista can be spiced up with members' voice and ONE. Let's look at the background. Ericsson is one of the world's largest manufacturers of mobile phones. Alta Vista is one of the largest search engines on the web. Both companies are global, but are both limited locally because they can only communicate in the local language.

The Internet is in the midst of rapid expansion when it comes to moving pictures and sound. An interesting field is translation functions that can translate basic internet information live. This can be developed so that everyone at ONE-AltaVista.com can be reached in the language that they prefer. This can be turned into a number of new opportunities.

"All communication is on the terms of the receiver. The problem is the number of terms."

The structure has been established for members' voice – "Communicate globally in one language to all languages."

This example shows the potential for mobile Internet to tear down language barriers. I'll leave the specific services and business models to the future.

Who would you call if you could send spoken e-mail to anyone in any country? How would this affect patterns of consumption? When do you think that there will be a ONE language for the entire world? Why one language? Why not?

Use the Powers That Be to Your Advantage

Federal Express delivers over 3 million parcels per working day. In the middle of September 2000, all of Paris was at a standstill due to a gas strike which had blocked all main roads. The local press reported the story day and night until journalists had said all there was to say. In search of a new angle, Robert my friend came up with an interesting thought: "Federal Express should make the most of the situation by delivering their packages on horseback in historical uniforms. History and romance mixed with the Parisians dramatic strike would give Federal Express the perfect forum to reach billions all over the world with the message "When everything grinds to a halt, Federal Express still delivers."

With Robert's kind permission I developed his thoughts further in my book. Do you see similar opportunities in the world today? (My example was purely symbolic with no bearing on the political situation.)

Cloning Celebrities

Brands, as we know, borrow not only from familiar symbols, but from celebrities as well. Below are a number of opportunities for cloning both celebrity and celebrities.

Factor 1: Celebrity

Dead or alive, cynicism or naiveté, celebrity will always be a strong factor in advertising.

Factor 2: Swedish Glass

Historical values are a hard sell on an increasingly competitive market. Old handcraft is losing added value on the market; the supply is greater than the demand. Consumers would rather buy mass-produced glass from Portugal than hand blown glass from Sweden.

Effect Factor 4

The product is given an individual charisma and becomes a strong brand.

In this example, we are going to create a product line that springs from the profile and image of Swedish glass while we help things along with a bit of celebrity. The line is based on strong tradition and identity. The basic idea is that traditional design must give way to bolder approaches to increased sales. One way is to let internationally famous Swedes bring the spotlight with them to Sundala Glassworks. First, we create a "Sunset Sundala", Sweden's equivalent of Sunset Boulevard. By developing an original design profile, the series can be marketed as "the boulevard of the home". A large percentage of the target group consists of collectors and celebrity buffs. The age of the group will fluctuate according to the celebrity. The product line of plates, glasses, and cup would be of media interest. The choice of media would also be steered by target group and celebrity. There is certainly no lack of magazines that would want to have the Graaf sisters, James Brown or Robbie Williams for dinner. By developing a product line with real value, PR can be carried out on a global scale. Internet, for example, can be a major factor in increasing sales.

There are risks in using celebrities in advertising, yet the potential profits that come from this kind of recognition mean that many companies are willing to take a chance.

As for the balance between handicraft and commercial interests, that's another subject all together.

COMMON SENSE IN BRANDING

Always listen to a good idea from anyone regardless of his or her job title. The idea is what is important. This is also a way to make your brand humble. Start with a new approach: talk to people who DO NOT work with branding. Simplicity is a great tool for common sense in branding. Use only basic words to describe your brand.

Regardless of the brand favored by customers, common sense remains a useful competitive tool. At a talk I recently gave to some 60-shoe store managers, I wore one brown and one white shoe. During the last 15 minutes of the talk I placed myself so the audience could not see my shoes. When I asked the participants to say what shoes I was wearing, 15 percent were able to say they were different. It makes you wonder how interested stores are in their customers. When asked how many wore their own brands, 30 percent acceded. It makes you wonder if people believe in their own product, and whether it is here, at the level of basic

values, that competition could become considerably more effective. Why not try similar tests in your own stores?

Here are two articles that are written for international business magazines, that shows how companies can work with sales and branding simultaneously using common sense.

Saab needs to go outside the car-box-branding

Many critics say that Saab needs to redesign the car model to be more different. Yes, that's true but more interesting; can branding knowledge be a part of product development? Why are brands interesting and products often boring? GM wants fast results, but redesigning takes time and is expensive. So let us look at ways for Saab to break the declining trend and sell more cars.

Use the values in the Swedish nation brand: Sweden needs Saab as a potent symbol and without the original brands, Sweden would more or less be a blond brand marketed by Hollywood.

The concept of nations as brands has long been accepted. Saab is using values (ie, safety, environment, quality, etc) from the nation brand. How can Sweden as a brand and Saab work together? For instance, all Saab owners worldwide should visit Sweden on the same day as a PR marketing campaign. Wherever a Saab owner is in the world, he or she should have a connection to Sweden. Why not offer a promotional trip to Sweden for the first 50,000 new car buyers? Also offer a special trip to 20,000 recent buyers of the latest Saab model. Develop the PR and branding for the car by collaborating with famous Saab owners. For instance, Bjorn Borg could drive a Saab across Europe back home to Sweden. You can work globally with this Saab tour by using the local sales and marketing forces. What an adventure you could create for local Saab owners from UK, Spain, USA, etc -- who can drive their Saab to Sweden? How wild will the local press drive the Saab brand? Maybe some newspaper headlines will be "The

Vikings are going back to Sweden, and their leader is Saab this time". Get the salespeople to listen to the consumer buzz on the street level and incorporate it with the marketing.

If Tiger Woods is driving and playing golf on the way to Sweden, then support the golf target group with the same model in PR and marketing. To support the tour, there should be a campaign site, www.saabadventure.com, on the internet where all the drivers can build a community. Every car should have a sticker with a unique number from 1-70,000. When people spot any of these cars on the street, they can go to the website and read about different family adventures, see photos, read their diary or send them questions about their car (this would make it easy for the press to follow the tour). Consumers can compete to win a brand new Saab by booking a free test drive on the internet.

If there is an average of three people in every of the 70,000 cars, the tour totals 210,000 Saab fans. If they use special printed postcards and community emails to send their stories from the trip to 20 friends, it will be about 4,200,000 people that will read and spread the word about the Saab story (why not send 10% of these to the CEOs of GM). Every week there is a top 10 story list on the site for reporters and fans to read and spread. To support the storytelling from the contenders, they should produce specially made car accessories.

Swedish tourism would be delighted with 210,000 people visiting and spending money in the country. Moreover, there could be millions of future tourists inspired by the publicity of the tour. How strong will this consumption of Sweden make the Saab brand? The brand values hidden behind the scene, usually not visible for consumers, need to be made visible. When you give a car a deeper identity and history, its buyers are less likely to change brand. And, isn't it true that most brands today within the car industry are considered "global brands", with no deeper identity?

In addition to profit on the sales of cars connected to the tour, Saab will have a lot of opportunities to gain extra income and additional values. For example, the tour could be partly financed by partners with matching brands, interested in the publicity and context of the adventure.

Here are some questions to develop the adventure tour:

How can they not only finance the adventure, but also make a profit? How can every sale of a trip to Sweden also communicate an offer from Saab? What other opportunities do you see on this tour?

This is only one example of how a company could recreate an identity lost in globalization by using their roots. Selling 200,000 cars is now a problem outside the car-box.

"With your positive outlook on Saab challenges and thoughts on our importance for Sweden you also contributes in a good way."
Knut Simonsson, Executive Director, Global Marketing, Saab Automobile

Soap your brand to success

Are you finding romance, comedy, or intrigue in the aisles of your local supermarket? If all you see are mushy peas and gray meat products, you are obviously not getting the ICA treatment.

Shopping for food is not the most exciting event in most people's lives. Faced with the need to build its brand as well as sell products, Swedish food retail chain ICA hit upon an entertaining way to promote itself and its products. Sweden's three dominant players, ICA, COOP and Axfood, account for about 90 percent of food retailing nationwide. Similar in offerings, ICA (a unit of the sinking Dutch-based international food retailer Ahold) hit upon an interesting concept to differentiate itself while still immersing the consumer in its products and services.

ICA's ongoing advertising campaign takes on

a short-story form set in local ICA stores where actors depict staff members and customers in real-life situations. The commercials create buzz, and people actively look forward to the next episode. In fact, the ads are so popular some of the actors have been elevated to national celebrity status. To finance the commercials, ICA allows other brands and products to co-brand episodes. The product offering is mirrored at ICA stores to create consistency with what the store is advertising and selling. This also gives branded products a chance to promote their wares on a level with ICA's large private-label selection.

From an internal branding viewpoint, the realistic settings and situations inspire staff and help build a passion for the company culture. Consistent with the themes and messages in the advertising vehicle, ICA compiled a comic book that depicted similar situations for an internal communications piece.

Of course, the challenge for ICA is how to make the in-store brand experience as exciting as the commercials. How can ICA ensure that the brand lives up to the communication? One idea would be for ICA to involve the customer more actively. Instead of merely watching the advertisements, customers could be invited to participate. Even if this only involves the person acting as a normal customer shopping for food, the excitement of involving everyday people would make the customer feel more actively involved in the brand.

About three million Swedes belong to ICA's customer loyalty program. ICA could reward and encourage these customers by allowing them to be stand-ins or act in the commercials. If they have an opportunity to act, mix with the product offerings and perhaps even earn extra points on their membership card, the momentum of brand promotion could be tremendous. Financing could come directly from co-branding sponsorship and product placement. And publicity could come from involving customers further, such as allowing them to vote for "best actor" online. ICA could also further develop its website to enhance communication, and in turn, its brand. Perhaps ICA could use the Internet as a collective think tank with possibilities for customers to be part of the creation of the commercials by directing their own episode or even recommending products to feature. This type of online involvement leads to further promotion of the brand.

4
Distribution Creates Added Value

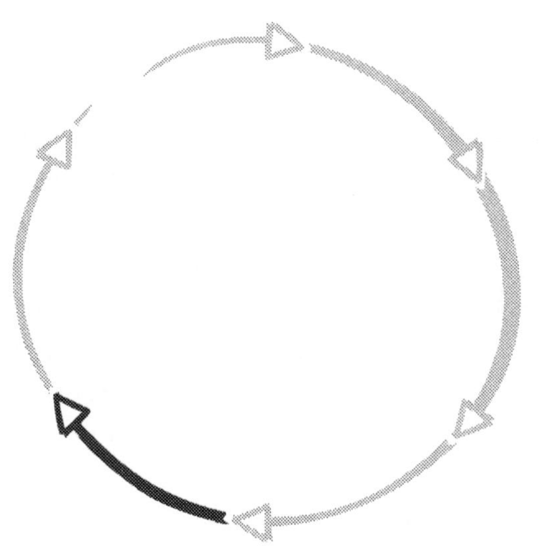

A distributor's power comes from the fact that he is closer to the customer at the point of sales than the supplier. Distribution is critical in reaching consumers with a brand. Large grocery chains are often left in the dust by fast food chains such as McDonald's.

Coca-Cola can be found everywhere, not because it's so popular. Rather, Coca-Cola is so popular because it can be found everywhere. The Coca-Cola company realized early on that by making sure their machines could be found in every corner of the world on every street, the choice of soft drink would be clear. And it is.

Success and oblivion can hang on how a product is distributed. If you can create an imbalance by pioneering a new form of distribution (such as Coca-Cola in the 1950's) you create new opportunities. If you want to dance, you have to move. The tango opens doors. Unfortunately, much on the market is far too stagnant. Far too many players are just standing around waiting for someone to ask them to dance.

Is there tango in your business?

What movement do you see on the market. What behavior causes new forms of consumption?

THE QUALITY OF LIFE – NEEDS/CONSUMPTION

No matter how much we surf digitally, we are still trapped on Maslow's stairway of needs. Distribution of our most important goods have yet to progress past the Neanderthal stage. Why should goods travel twice around the world before they meet the consumer? Why must every family carry milk and detergent every year equivalent to the weight of five elephants? The perpetual rush to get things done lowers the quality of life. The market always has a solution, such as home delivery and website orders. The problem of goods having to travel around the world, however, remains. The means of distribution should be closer to the consumer.

Two businesses that have succeeded in creating good local distribution are insurance and cable TV. They have managed to sell their services directly to employers and landlords. A slight rent increase pays for the extra channels. Why couldn't the same sort of increase pay for stocking the laundry room with detergent? Why not offer milk and Coca-Cola on tap in every apartment?

Since the original Swedish language version of this book was printed, Coca-Cola has announced plans to begin distributing their beverage by pipeline.

"IT may be just a pipe dream, but Douglas Daft, the chief executive of Coca-Cola, is planning to compete with water by channelling Coke through taps in customers' homes". Interview by Rupert Steiner, Sunday Times.

There is nothing so rewarding as being ahead of your time.

Another solution could be a "brand card" – a sort of credit card for a brand that registers consumption of distributed goods to the end consumer. The brand card could identify different lifestyles, stimulate consumption and help aim different messages at different target groups.

Entertainment and social values can be developed from the ground up; in the end only the circus will remain. Why not let the circus sell the goods directly?

Using the entertainment and recreation industry as a sales force, the social network for different groups of consumers can bring people closer; for example, boating enthusiasts, golfers, outdoorsmen, etc. When consumption is part of the actual activity, a strong emotional bond is formed with the product.

The experience associated with the sale, becomes a part of the value of the brand.

Go back to section I, chapter 1. Choose something from your surroundings and develop it. How does distribution affect the power scenario?

LIVING – LIFESTYLE: "BRAND LIVING"

Our relationship to all of the roles we play in life can be improved substantially by a skillful "director". The corporate world can become our life's theater. Consumers spend their money on products with added value. A clear trend: how we live is becoming more and more of a lifestyle that can be shaped by those who succeed in convincing the consumer of its value. Housing of the future will be more focused on "lifestyle living" where real estate developers and landlords offer a ready-made lifestyle that contains the "right" emotional undertones. Certain brand combinations are stronger than the sum of their parts. The consumer is playing a sort of part in a lifelong commercial played for himself and those around him. "Others offer housing, we offer a lifestyle" and "buy yourself" will be the ad slogans of the future.

The hotel business must be full of know-how and even developed concepts of this type that could be invaluable for companies interested in creating this new way of living.

What opportunities do you see in your company? Discuss and develop.

A brand that has really given brand living a home on wheels is Harley Davidson, a brand that made advertising history. Harley Davidson is also a great example of a company and its customers working together. The company's quality problems didn't ruin the company thanks to the strength of the Harley myth. The company began listening to its customers and learned how they should further develop their product. They went on Harley Davidson meets and saw what their customers wanted and what needed to be done to improve their product. Harley Davidson became ONE with the customer. It took awhile, but the company went from near bankruptcy to a modern branding miracle. When customers tattoo Harley Davidson on their arms and wear their logo on their clothes, they are merely showing their uniform as employees of Harley Davidson-ONE.

What visible symbols can your customers carry and develop for your company? The Harley front wheel fork is a classic case of how customers have helped to develop a product. What is the corresponding product for your company?

In 2000, the German world champion Sven Ottke defended his title live on EuroSport in front an audience of millions. He had an enormous tattooed web address on his back. Who was the real winner in this match?

If you were given a 25% raise would you tattoo your company's name on your arm? What company will break into the limelight with "skin-deep" advertising?

5
Putting Ideas Into Action

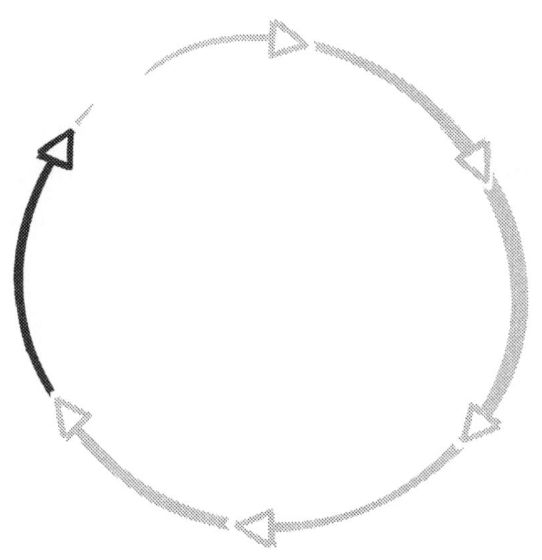

So far, you've studied Detective Marketing's potential and learned its finer points. Now it's time to put it into action. There is a special model for doing this.

The value of the creative meeting increases when ideas are put to work. Often, a limited budget raises the level of creativity. (There are times, however, when it can be a limitation as well...) Try to start working on the ideas without looking at the budget. Save the calculations until you've refined your ideas. Detective Marketing's strength is in its simplicity; it can easily be used by many different departments. Change and growth should be seen long-term, especially anything having to do with education. Using Detective Marketing gives a broader perspective and creates mental profit.

HISTORY – THE FUTURE

One of history's great visionaries was writer and civil servant Niccolò Machiavelli (1469 – 1527). In my opinion, he was one of the first consultants in the art of shaping attitudes. One of his great skills was communicating complicated concepts in understandable terms. His solutions were based on a thorough analysis of what the target group wanted to hear. Here is my loose interpretation of the master's insights.

Putting ideas into action is based on three steps:

1. Timing
2. The value of the product
3. Context

These three steps have many synonyms. The ability to work together as a team is reflected in the end result. Opportunities are proportional to teamwork. Match the characteristics that are best suited to steps 1-3. There are no rules as to the interplay of these characteristics. Your imagination is the only referee. Remember, the sum of the parts should be an easily communicated whole. Then, use the magnifying glass to see where your efforts should be concentrated.

Timing

When will your efforts have the greatest impact?

Characteristics: Weather, new legislation, changing attitudes. When are our competitors least visible in the media? When is the next baby boom? What trends can we see? What environmental arguments apply at the present time?

Seasons, holidays and pay-days – "*time to cash in*".

When does your company have its "time to cash in" and can this affect be maximized.

The hardest sell is the present. Today is the future.

The Value of the Product

What are the product's added values (meta-product)?

Characteristics: Why does the product or service exist? How can it be further developed to make it more unique? In what category should it be positioned; that is, in what context should it be seen? With a limited budget, it can be better to create a new category.

In what areas does the product have strong added value? How can you sell the qualities of the product instead of just the product itself? What values are relevant for the target group? The price is part of the product; discuss how you can create values through pricing.

Context

Machiavelli identified the human need to see things in a larger pattern. Where does the consumer see the most logic in your message/product? Choose a relevant context where you will have the greatest impact. The choice can also be interpreted as how you intend to position your product. Where is my message most appropriate and where on the field am I most likely to make the most goals?

Characteristics: Media planning should naturally take into consideration things such as the reader of a periodical and the target group for the advertised product.

Example 1: Use the trade press, special inserts and TV programs that work together to create an environment where the target group is most open to your message. Sometimes it is necessary to talk to the consumer in a world slightly removed from the daily media static, for example in the morning paper. Direct mail is also an option. By creating consistently high visibility in the mailbox, a company can create its own context.

Example 2: Contemporary and cozy room furnishings at IKEA and in its catalog, gives each of its products added value by placing it in a context. Product lines, matching textiles, furniture, accessories – everything is set in a context and is part of an attractive concept. How and where can your business create this sort of added value?

Example 3: How can you highlight the relationship between your product and the consumer's identity? Characteristics (implicit and explicit) can work together between steps 1-3. This interplay can be very successful by creating the right inner tension.

Remember: All wrong can be all right. In fact, all wrong can be great!

The examples in this book are all based on these three steps. Study them and you will soon see the pattern. Variations on this model are endless!

6
Let's Keep In Touch

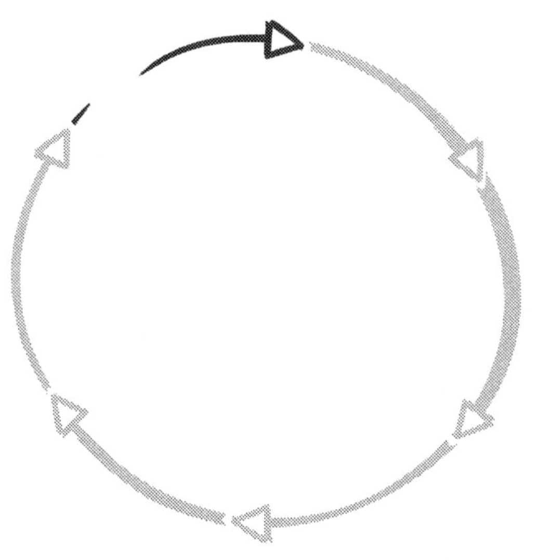

Everything must come full circle. This book, however, is based on a circle made of two-way communication. The book doesn't end with this chapter, it goes on with you, the reader. Just as the end-user of a product or service is the best authority on how to improve it and find new uses for it, you, the reader are the best person to further develop my method.

Time for You to Take Over

This book continues on my website where you and other readers can further develop the method and exchange ideas and experiences. The site is a neutral meeting place where everyone can get along regardless of corporate affiliation, business or title.

Visitors' opinions and comments will be collected and published in a newsletter that will be sent to all registered members. It is my hope that the site will become a place for new thinking, contacts and workshops. The site will also serve as a means of contacting this student of life for lectures or consulting.

A thousand thoughts without communication lead nowhere. Please take part.

Meetings give birth to the riches of learning.

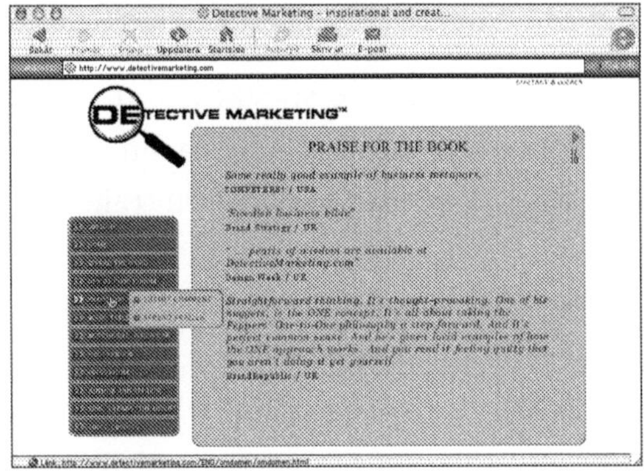

Afterword

People with a wealth of ideas need mentors not only for nourishment and advice, but also to cut and trim when the ideas grow wild. I am very grateful for the guidance my meetings with my mentors have given me. In this book I am my own iceberg; my friends ask questions to keep the book from melting...

A Few Words About the Spirit of Creativity

According to modern science, man had developed the mental capacity for speech long before he started to use it. I think we also have an undeveloped spiritual capacity. Native cultures used spirituality as a natural part of everyday life. Creativity is a way of making contact with the spiritual world. The child in you has that ability. This is not science speaking, but rather my intuition. It is we alone who set the limits for how far that which has yet to be done can take us.

A Few Words About Self-Criticism

My method is an on-going process. Tomorrow's experiences will allow me to improve future editions of this book. I value your opinions and so do other readers of this book. Open your senses and see yourself as a factor in these examples. Read them again now and then for inspiration.

"The grass is always greener on both sides of the hill." This is true for all kinds of knowledge. It is essential to meet with both new knowledge and good ol' ignorance.

My hope is that this book will be the beginning of your road to success. Maybe I'll meet you along the way at *www.detectivemarketing.com*

P.S. When it comes to models and methods: Never confuse the dance you are dancing with the fact you're dancing.

YOUR COMMENTS ON THIS BOOK

www.detectivemarketing.com

READING LIST

Armstrong and Kotler, *Principles of Marketing* (1994): Prentice Hall International

Autry, *Love and Profit : The Art of Caring Leadership* (1992): Avon Books

Branson, *Losing my Virginity: The Authorized Biography* (1998): Virgin Publishing

Berglind (ed.), *Skapande ögonblick: Psykodrama och sociodrama* (1998)

Börrefors and Welin, *Från idé till kommersiell succé* (1986)

Cameron, *The Artist's Way* (1992): J P Tarcher

Cederquist, *Reklown - 30 år i reklamens manege* (1997)

Dahlgren and Szatek, *Marknadsförnyelse* (1998)

Dyson, *Release 2.1: A Design for Living in the Digital Age* (2001): Broadway Books

Falonius and Hedberg, *Spelet på marknaden* (1997)

Foley, *Varför människan blev människa: en antropologisk studie av mänsklighetens tidiga evolution* (1998)

Frankelius, *Kirurgisk marknadsföring* (1997)

Frankelius and Rosén, *Företaget och omvärlden* (1994)

Godin, *Unleashing the Ideavirus* (2000): Simon & Schuster

Goldmann, *How to Win Customers* (1993): Pan Books

Gregerman, *Lessons from the Sandbox* (2000): Contemporary Books

Gustafsson and Rennemark, *Reklam som säljer* (1990)

Jansson, *Första boken* (1994)

Jung, *Man and His Symbols* (1997): Laureleaf

Klein Naomi, *No Logo: Taking Aim at the Brand Bullies* (2000): Picador USA. Flamingo UK.

Klein, *Ateisten och den heliga staden* (1987)

Land and Jarman, *Breakpoint and Beyond. Mastering the Future Today* (1998): Leadership 2000 Inc.

Lindahl, *Ett produktivt förhållningssätt* (1992)

Linn, *Metaprodukten och marknaden* (1985)

Linn, *Brand Dynamics* Inst for Brand Leadership (1998)

Maslow, *Motivation and Personality* Addison-Wesley (1987)

Melin, *Varumärket som strategiskt konkurrensmedel.* Lund University Studies in Economics and Management (1997)

Peppers, *The One to One Fieldbook* (1999): Bantam Books

Rackham, *Spin Selling* (1998): McGraw-Hill

Selin, *Svenska massmedier* (1995)

Wahlström, *Efter stålbadet* (1994)

Zukav, *The Dancing Wu Li Masters* (1994): Bantam Books

ACKNOWLEDGEMENTS

I would like to thank everyone who has given me support, enthusiasm and advice on this interactive book. I would first like to thank to my girlfriend and my life. My mother, brothers and family for being there. Rosengård, Dallas, Henri, Jan Cederquist, Jonas Nilsson, Gertie, Ulf, Nicolai, Magnus & Max Eriksson, Niclas, Ib, Bo, Stefan, Ola, Marianne, Lina, Jörgen Wahl, Lars, Stuart, Michael, Lennart, Barbro, Robert, Fredik, Gudrun, Öresundskomiteen, Bengt Jönsson, Eva, Bo, Camilla, Karin, Erik, Mats, Frisco, Irini, Sergej, Merci Robles, Ilene, Carl Fredrik & Marie. Ulla & Stig.

As someone suffering from dyslexia when I wrote the original book in Swedish, a patient interpreter of the caliber of Katarina Frigell can be compared to an angel.

Credits: Jerry Bengtsson, Reklam & Design-historiska Föreningen / Ib Thaning. Elisabet Heinbürger, KPA / Johan Larsson, Mattsson& Friends. Gunilla Steinwall, Non-Smoking Generation. WWF / Aggeborgs. Kent Melin, HIFI Art. Claes Andréasson, The Absolut Company. Vice Precident: Mitch Lazar, CNN. President: Pierre Paperon, Alta Vista. Johan Hjelm, ICA / King. Saab, Knut Simonsson, Executive Director, Global

Marketing. TOMPETERS! Al Ries, chairman, Ries & Ries. Forsling & Flyborg Universal Music. J.Nordwall Design / Joachim Nordwall. Nofont / Andreas Carlsson. Light My Fire.

The Nokia Ads and products are made up examples to show how to use the methodology of the book. The Nokia name and trademark belongs to the Nokia Company.

All trademarks in this book are acknowledged as belonging to their respective companies.

Thanks to the legendary Steve Strid for translating, adapting and re-working the materialin this book for the US and English-speaking market. Thanks to Per Nilsson for help with re-worked chapter common sense in branding. Thanks to everyone that has given me inspiration and spread the wild flights of fancy that I have collected in this living book.

And without my friends anxiety and procrastination, this book would never have been possible.

BIOGRAPHY

After finishing his studies in economics, Stefan Engeseth pursued a career as a professional dancer. In his spare time, he read books on management, innovation and marketing, an interest that eventually led to the creation of his own related theories and concepts. He contacted several of the top authors in each field to share his ideas and comment on their work. Some of his contributions ended up in their books and soon he was asked to write a book of his own. Three years later, Detective Marketing, was finished followed by two English language editions.

Stefan's ideas range from innovative and future-oriented to bordering on far-fetched. Yet, they all build on the universal truth that without innovation and visions, companies will not grow in today's highly competitive business world. The question is, how far are you prepared to go? Stefan uses scenarios from companies such as CNN, Sony, GM, Coca-Cola, Nokia and Ericsson to illustrate the enormous potential of all companies.

Stefan has always been fascinated by the detective's endless search for clues and answers. He has used interviews with real working detectives to formulate theories for the business world. Detective

Marketing presents his method of finding what's hidden in the blind spot and learning to see what your competitors don't. The detective finds your customers' hidden needs and helps the marketer communicate it. Set aside a pleasant hour or two to let yourself get inspired by Detective Marketing. Who knows what you will come up with.

Stefan has been called everything from consultant to chaos pilot. A well-known lecture and writer, Stefan has built a solid reputation as a sort of "Jonathan Livingston Seagull" of the business world. Over the years, he has worked with such diverse companies as Letsbuyit.com and the Swedish Postal Service.

He has held over 500 lectures and workshops internationally at corporations and academic institutions attended by the University of Stockholm, Pace University (New York), Associations of Advertisers and Marketing Federations in different countries.

He has also taken part in the Öresund bridge between Sweden and Denmark one of the largest projects of its kind in Europe. He write articles for international business magazines (Brand Republic, In-Store Marketing, Brand Strategy, Brand Channel etc).

www.ingramcontent.com/pod-product-compliance
Ingram Content Group UK Ltd.
Pitfield, Milton Keynes, MK11 3LW, UK
UKHW040007200726
13854UKWH00001B/87